JOURNAL OF AMERICAN INDIAN EDUCATION

Volume 54, Number 2
Summer 2015

The *Journal of American Indian Education* (ISSN 0021-8731) is published three times a year in spring, summer, and fall by the University of Minnesota Press, 111 Third Avenue South, Suite 290, Minneapolis, MN 55401-2520. http://www.upress.umn.edu

Postmaster: Send address changes to *JAIE*, University of Minnesota Press, 111 Third Avenue South, Suite 290, Minneapolis, MN 55401-2520.

Inquiries about manuscript submissions should be sent to jaie@asu.edu. Further information about manuscript submission is in the back of this issue and available online at http://www.upress.umn.edu/journal-division/Journals/journal-of-american-indian-education/editorial-information

Address subscription orders, changes of address, and business correspondence (including requests for permission and advertising orders) to *JAIE*, University of Minnesota Press, 111 Third Avenue South, Suite 290, Minneapolis, MN 55401-2520.

Subscriptions: Regular U.S. rates: individuals, 1 year (three issues) $35; libraries, 1 year $75. Other countries add $5 for each year's subscription. Checks should be made payable to the University of Minnesota Press. Back issues published after 2014: $20 (plus $6 shipping for the first copy, $1.25 for each additional copy inside the United States; $9.50 shipping for the first copy, $6 for each additional copy outside the United States). Back issues published before 2015: Please contact jaie@asu.edu.

Digital subscriptions to the *Journal of American Indian Education* are available online through the JSTOR Current Scholarship Program at http://www.jstor.org/r/umnpress.

JOURNAL OF AMERICAN INDIAN EDUCATION

VOLUME 54, ISSUE 2 2015

Editors' Introduction

WELCOME TO THE SECOND ISSUE of the *Journal of American Indian Education* produced by our new publishing partner, the University of Minnesota Press. We are very pleased to have the professional support and expertise of the press's staff. As our readers may have noticed in the past few months, the press is now handling journal subscriptions and renewals. To sign up or renew your subscription, please visit the University of Minnesota Press website for *JAIE* at http://www.upress.umn.edu/journal-division/Journals/journal-of-american-indian-education.

We are also happy to report that the journal is updating our own website, with able assistance from the technical support staff of the School of Social Transformation at Arizona State University. Hopefully, by the time this issue goes to press, the new site will be up and running or soon to appear. The URL for the Center for Indian Education remains the same; you can find us at http://center-for-indian-education.asu.edu. One important feature of the new site will be a functioning link to apply to serve as a peer reviewer for the journal. We depend upon our colleagues in the field for this important professional service and look forward to an efficient way for you to let us know your willingness to serve. We apologize for the frustrations some of you have experienced with the old website; we realized only recently that the site was so outdated that the page with the application form for signing up as a peer reader was no longer working.

We are proud of this issue's balance of two feature articles and two *Reports from the Field,* all of which share a passionate and personal commitment to enriching and sustaining the quality of Indigenous education. In "Remembering Their Words, Evoking Kiŋuniivut: The Development of the Iñupiaq Learning Framework," two Iñupiaq educators, Pausauraq Jana Harcharek and Cathy Tagnak Rexford, share deeply personal narratives of their journeys as they engaged "community members on Alaska's North Slope in healing, visioning, and committing to bringing Iñupiaq knowledge back to the forefront." Their powerful reflections inspire us with the intellectual integrity and generous spirit at the heart of Indigenous peoples and Indigenous knowledge systems.

Ananda Marin and Megan Bang also use narrative in the processes of "storywork" as they chronicle and analyze the ways in which American Indian teachers design pedagogies for Indigenous science education. Working with elders, teachers, parents, youth, community content experts, and content professionals at one of the oldest and largest urban Indian centers in the United States, the authors offer a compelling model of community-based research designed to reclaim classrooms for Indigenous teaching and learning.

Matthew Etherington's *Report from the Field* on "Aboriginal Perspectives and Issues in Teacher Education" confronts the challenges of effectively and humanely training non-Aboriginal teachers in Canada for respectful, competent engagement with Aboriginal histories, communities, and students. Etherington describes a course for fourth-year preservice teachers that integrated Aboriginal Elders and encouraged personal transformation through a performance examination that the Elders evaluated. Aboriginal leaders who consulted on the course design suggested that, in order to achieve course goals, "some suffering would be required" of the preservice teachers. Etherington's brilliant analysis of the course dynamics develops a critical distinction between the preservice teachers' understandings of "justice" versus "benevolence."

In the issue's second *Report from the Field*, a project to develop an undergraduate social work degree based in tribal communities required collaboration across the Turtle Mountain Band of Chippewa Indians and the Standing Rock Sioux Tribe, Turtle Mountain Community College and Sitting Bull College, and the University of North Dakota. Coauthors Heitkamp, Vermillion, Flanagan, and Nedegaard report how using a nation-building framework successfully guided the collaboration, as nation building and social work share the core value of community self-determination. They describe seven principles they found effective in developing a culturally responsive social work education program for, with, and in Indigenous communities.

We hope you enjoy this exciting issue of *JAIE*!

Warm regards,

Bryan McKinley Jones Brayboy, K. Tsianina Lomawaima, and Teresa L. McCarty, Editors

IN MEMORIAM

Joshua A. (Shikl) Fishman

JULY 18, 1926–MARCH 1, 2015

ON MARCH 1, 2015, the world lost one of the greatest sociolinguists and minority-language advocates of our time, Joshua A. (Shikl) Fishman. Known for his prolific writings on the sociology of language (more than 1,000 articles and monographs) and especially for his work on the protection and promotion of minoritized languages, Dr. Fishman was a strong and highly effective ally in the fight to revitalize and maintain Indigenous languages. "[U]nabashedly in favor of bilingual education," he believed that "bilingual education urgently requires not only attention and understanding but also sympathy, assistance and dedication" (Fishman, 1976, as cited in García, Peltz, Schiffman, & Fishman, 2006, p. 15).

Dr. Fishman was present at the second Stabilizing Indigenous Languages Symposium held at Northern Arizona University in May 1995, where he famously advised those in attendance that schools "should be on tap and not on top of a language. The language does not belong to them. The language makes use of them" (Fishman, 1996, p. 194). Above all, Fishman insisted, schools should work in tandem with families and communities to safeguard the cradle of heritage language maintenance: intergenerational mother tongue transmission in the home. Further, he encouraged, "it *is* possible for small groups of . . . individuals to re-arrange their lives individually and collectively exactly in this revolutionary way" (1996, p. 194). Dr. Fishman would know, for that is precisely what he and his life partner of more than 60 years, Gella Schweid Fishman, did with Yiddish in their own Bronx, New York, home. As he recalled in a 1996 interview with Teresa McCarty, as a child at the dinner table, his father would ask his children, "What did you do for the language [Yiddish] today?" Joshua and Gella made Yiddish the language of their home and, with a few like-minded Yiddish-speaking families, the language of their close urban neighborhood. He urged Native American parents and educators to do the same with

Joshua and Gella Fishman in their Bronx, New York, home, February 2010. Photograph by Teresa L. McCarty.

their heritage mother tongues. "*Do not* leave your language alone," Fishman cautioned in a book by the same title (2006). "Reversing language shift . . . is community building," he emphasized; "that is what is essentially required, in and through the beloved language" (1996, p. 196).

Joshua and Gella Fishman traveled widely and conducted several tours of Navajo and other Native nations to speak with educators, tribal leaders, and community members on language revitalization and maintenance. He participated in the National Association for Bilingual Education's "reversing Indigenous language shift" sessions, and he held a 1998 summer residency at the American Indian Language Development Institute at the University of Arizona, where he taught a course based on his classic book, *Reversing Language Shift* (Fishman, 1991). "One thing we can be sure of," Fishman insisted, is that "those who do not give up, but try again and again, become a community of hope, a community of dedication" (1996, p. 196). But, he added, hope must be met with an equal portion of action—not for the language itself, "but for the lifestyle"—the relationships and cultural world to which language is intimately tied (1996, p. 195).

And that is perhaps the greatest gift that Joshua Fishman has left us—hope for the future of Indigenous and other "smaller" oppressed languages and the wisdom and tools through which to construct that future. In what follows, we share a personal tribute to Joshua Fishman by Dr. Tiffany S. Lee, who reflects on his impact on her own language loyalties and his legacy for students of American Indian education and Indigenous/Native American studies.

Respectfully,

The Editors

REFERENCES

Fishman, J. A. (1991). *Reversing language shift: Theoretical and empirical foundations of assistance to threatened languages.* Clevedon, United Kingdom: Multilingual Matters.

Fishman, J. A. (1996). Maintaining languages: What works? What doesn't? In G. Cantoni (Ed.), *Stabilizing Indigenous languages* (pp. 186–198). Flagstaff: Northern Arizona University Center for Excellence in Education.

Fishman, J. A. (2006). *DO NOT leave your language alone: The hidden status agendas within corpus planning in language policy.* Mahwah, NJ: Erlbaum.

García, O., Peltz, R., Schiffman, H., & Fishman, G. S. (2006). *Language loyalty, continuity and change: Joshua A. Fishman's contributions to international sociolinguistics.* Clevedon, United Kingdom: Multilingual Matters.

Beyond Sociolinguistics: Joshua Fishman's Influence on Students in Native American Studies

TIFFANY S. LEE

I MET DR. FISHMAN while I was a graduate student at Stanford University, and he spent the winter months there teaching for the School of Education. Of course, I knew of him prior to this time, not just because of his prolific work on heritage-language issues but because of his impact on my family. My uncle, Wayne Holm, and my late aunt Agnes Holm, both former educators at Rock Point Community School on the Navajo Nation, would tell me stories of his visit to Rock Point and the impact of his work on American Indian language education. So I felt very honored and excited to have the opportunity to take courses with Dr. Fishman at Stanford.

I learned about language maintenance, connections to identity, language shift, and the politics of language across linguistic contexts worldwide. Having the eternally inquisitive mind, Dr. Fishman would call on me to personally discuss with him the language politics, change, shift, and connections to identity among Navajo people and communities. He challenged me to think deeply and critically about various theories and experiences related to language change and revitalization. I cannot express in words the level of impact he had on my research, thinking, learning, and personal connection to language revitalization research.

I have tried to extend the influence Dr. Fishman had on my learning to my students in Native American Studies (NAS) at the University of New Mexico (UNM). I teach a course titled Language Recovery, Revitalization, and Renewal in Native American Communities. It is a popular course among Native students at UNM because of the close relationship students feel between language and identity and because of the language change and shift they observe and experience in their own communities. Dr. Fishman understood that connection and wrote about it. Although he was a Jewish man of another generation and experienced the world from a completely different place than my students, his academic and personal writings have personally and meaningfully connected with my students, their learning, and the connections they make to their own communities' linguistic situations. For example, I have had students read the speeches he gave at the Stabilizing Indigenous Languages conferences (e.g., Cantoni, 1996). His speeches are personal essays imbued with academic content and humor. In one essay titled "What Do You Lose When You Lose Your Language?," he discussed the relationship between language and culture and how those who study language (outsiders) examine this relationship and what the people of the language (insiders) think about it. He said of this relationship:

> It is not a perfect relationship. Every language grows; every culture changes. Some words hang on after they are no longer culturally active. "Little Miss Muffet sat on a tuffet eating her curds and whey." Well, who knows what a tuffet is any more, and you cannot find anybody who knows what curds and whey are any more without doing research. Those are frozen traces. Even if there is often a good relationship between the words of the language and the concerns of the culture, there are more important relationships between language and culture than the indexical one. (Fishman, 1996, p. 81)

His speech continued to share how people talk about this relationship in different terms when asked about it. He said people talk about their language in terms of its sanctity, its importance for kinship, and their sense of moral responsibility to it. These ideas fall completely in line with what NAS students have shared regarding the relationship of language and culture in Native contexts. In our class discussions, students relay their familial experiences with language, change, and the importance of language and culture to students' sense of belonging, identity, and community. The words Dr. Fishman uses, through humor and passion, have moved NAS students because they can relate to his sentiments, his words, and his commitment to language revitalization. One student shared this comment in an online post about Dr. Fishman's writing: "This touched my heart and mind immensely. It is . . . hard to describe the utmost holiness of a language."

Although the NAS students did not meet Dr. Fishman in person, his influence has been tremendous. He has moved their spirits, as he did mine. I was able to visit him at his Bronx, New York, home in 2008. It was an experience I will never forget. Gella, his wife, was so gracious and inviting, and Dr. Fishman was his usual self as I knew him—kind and inquisitive about the Navajo language and the cultural and communal context as it existed at that point in time. Gella was preparing his papers and organizing his writings for later distribution. Her devotion to him was clear and palpable. We went to lunch at a local kosher deli. It was a warm and wonderful afternoon with two amazing human beings.

I will always treasure the time I had to learn from Dr. Fishman and my fond memories. I hope to continue to convey his devotion and his allegiance for heritage languages with my students in NAS. We have so much to learn from Dr. Fishman's life work. His passion, commitment, and dedication to heritage language revitalization live on through his words and our memories.

Tiffany S. Lee *(Dibé Łizhiní [Blacksheep Diné] and Oglala Lakota) is associate professor in Native American Studies at the University of New Mexico and former president of the Navajo Studies Conference, Inc. Board of Directors.*

REFERENCES

Cantoni, G. (Ed.). (1996). *Stabilizing Indigenous languages.* Flagstaff: Northern Arizona University Center for Excellence in Education.

Fishman, J. A. (1996). What do you lose when you lose your language? In G. Cantoni (Ed.), *Stabilizing Indigenous languages* (pp. 80–91). Flagstaff: Northern Arizona University Center for Excellence in Education.

Remembering Their Words, Evoking Kiŋuniivut: The Development of the Iñupiaq Learning Framework

PAUSAURAQ JANA HARCHAREK
and CATHY TAGNAK REXFORD

This article describes a community-led process to develop the Iñupiaq Learning Framework. In a narrative approach to sharing knowledge, two Iñupiaq educators chronicle their inspiration, motivation, and continued determination to claim Iñupiaq knowledge as the focus of learning. We present findings from an inquiry designed to engage community members on Alaska's North Slope in healing, visioning, and committing to bringing Iñupiaq knowledge back to the forefront. The narrative includes steps to current practice that can inform Native communities engaged in curricular reform.

The Story of the Iñupiaq Learning Framework Is a Story About Healing

Cathy Tagnak Rexford's Story

This is a story about healing. I was named after my great-grandmother, my grandfather's mother. Tagnak. Tagnak is what most people on the North Slope call me. But the less frequently used name, the name that gives me the strength to sustain the work I have to do in the world, was given to me by my grandmother. A name that I have not quite grown into that belongs to my great-aunt: Niġukkaiyaaq.

For you who are reading this, I ask that you hold this name in your minds and hearts as I begin to share

Pausauraq Jana Harcharek's Story

This is a story about healing, healing within the Iñupiaq Nation of the North Slope of Alaska.

It began with the advent of "schools," buildings usually located on the outskirts of communities where our children went to be "taught"—we thought—how to live. Schooling, a totally strange concept, meant that children no longer spent the days with parents, grandparents, aunts, uncles, and extended family learning how to be human beings as they went along in life. In school buildings, they were reflections of heaviness. Allow Niġukkaiyaaq's spirit to hold you as she has held me through times of unbelievable pain; allow her to guide us both. This is my own story—a story that both belongs to me and does not belong to me. It is just a simple story of healing. I tell you this because we need to begin this story together.

We need to begin this story in the right way. We need to begin this story with a prayer. And in this prayer, we need to acknowledge the spirit that has guided us together. We need to acknowledge the same breath of life that fills our bodies and binds us to this earth. We need to ask for the presence of our ancestors so that they may also heal and grieve our losses. In our prayer, let us open those parts of our hearts, spirits, minds, and bodies that are holding this heaviness and free ourselves. In our prayer, let us acknowledge that we are all a part of something bigger than we have words for. Let us breathe in that connection and align ourselves and feel the peace and the space it will bring. Let us begin. Let us begin together.

The awakening that I experienced began at the age of 17. I began writing poems about the beginning of time. I saw vividly powerful scenes, scenes from life as the Iñupiat had been living since our memories began, and I knew that reaching back into history was inspired by something bigger than myself. It was the first time I heard the voice that connects me to my lineage.

It was those poems, it seemed, that opened the doors instantly to a history that one can only describe as miraculous. That we have always found ways to survive against odds

told that speaking their language was bad; these negative messages worked to deter them forever from the path of becoming full human beings. During this era, many of our rituals, ceremonies, and celebrations were abandoned while learning the white man's ways, for times were changing, and we needed to be prepared for what was to come.

Then came the boarding-school era when children, sometimes as young as 5 years old, were taken away from their families and homes, fostering yet a deeper and darker chasm. Our children spent years in boarding schools when they should have been learning how to fully function in Iñupiaq society. The years parents were forced to be away from their children were lonely years, and when their children finally came home, they were not the same. They came home unable to speak in the language and knew naught about surviving in the extreme environment of their ancestors.

This new generation came home unprepared to live as Iñupiat and to raise children of their own in the ways of the Iñupiat. They had endured the pain and the hurt of being forced to speak English. They had become young adults in sterile environments devoid of feeling, environments where their parents and extended family were absent. They were victims of the Bureau of Indian Affairs (BIA) attitude that Native children were capable of learning only so much.

This generation would not, could not, inflict on their own children the same pain and suffering to which they had been subject. As a result of the forced assimilationist tactics per-

that are as slim as the stick that strikes the Eskimo drum is due to a combination of hard work, fortitude, and perseverance over generations.

As I grew up, I was encouraged to learn, encouraged to explore the world, and encouraged to ask questions. But there was a part of me that I felt lacked a language, lacked acknowledgment, and lacked energy. Later, I realized that it was my disconnection from *iñua*. I was raised primarily in cities, removed from connections to land, removed from the Iñupiaq language, and removed from understandings of traditional teachings. But a millennium of generational knowledge was still in my mind, heart, body, and spirit.

I began to feel the power of iñua, and as soon as I did, I committed myself to creating opportunities for it to grow, for it to be given its proper respect, and for it to work its way through my life in whichever way it chose.

The only way I can describe what happened in the following 15 years is that my ancestors began to trust me enough to work in education and in storytelling. Stories that come from the source of our strength, knowledge that has been crafted over generations, polished like an ivory carving, became the work outlined here, the work that is our collective birthright. But the journey along the way was hard. I carried and continue to carry heaviness, shame, anger, fear, and grief because to this day I cannot speak my language, cannot navigate the mountains near the village of Kaktovik, cannot properly care for animals that are caught by hunters, and cannot sew proper winter attire for the men in my family.

petrated by the BIA, they were the first generation to raise English-speaking children. Scores of individuals came back angry at a world that would inflict such inhumane practices on innocent young human beings. They were the generation deprived of a loving, nurturing home and caring community environment where the entire community took responsibility for raising children. Many of this generation turned to alcohol to mask the emotional pain and heartache they suffered. They did not feel at home in their own communities when they came home. They could not speak the language, and they did not know the intricacies and nuances of hunting, making appropriate clothing, or taking care of animals.

Several generations later, the cycle of social troubles that emanated from this disruption of social harmony continues to plague our people. Many of us blame the alcohol and the drugs that cause so much disorder in our communities for our discontent, restlessness, and general unhappiness in life. How many have said that the reason we cannot get ahead in life is because of drugs and alcohol—that alcohol and drugs are the culprit behind why we are so despondent and continue to depend on government and regional corporation handouts?

I believe that the social ills we face today incorporate the aftermath of an educational policy when language was oppressed, customary coming-of-age rituals were left to history, traditional religion and spirituality were abandoned, ceremonies were left to the wisps of the wind, and our children were sent away. Our minds were

(Cathy Tagnak Rexford, continued)

As I become more and more aware of the reasons why, I see a series of events that would be unbelievable if we had not experienced them directly. If our children had not been sent to boarding schools; if outside disease and sicknesses had not decimated families and villages; if our traditional spiritual practices had not been replaced by Christianity; if oil had not been discovered and drilled; and if our political, economic, and cultural systems had not been changed in the period of 100 years, this story we are creating together would not exist.

To hold this knowledge and this awareness in your being, to acknowledge it, and to simply say that it is true and that we survived it is extremely difficult to do. To acknowledge further that so many ways of knowing, seeing, and experiencing the world through traditional practice and language are near the edge of extinction—to acknowledge that we are on the cusp of losing our birthright—is perhaps even more difficult because our own personal actions or nonactions are woven into the story. We become a part of the equation. We step into the roles of our ancestors. To acknowledge the impacts of this heaviness and to see the ways we absorb the intergenerational stress is perhaps the most difficult of all. Through this struggle, the visions and the teachings that our ancestors have carried for thousands of years transform from theory into accessible knowledge. Together, we address this transformation in this article and replace our heaviness with the light and the joy of learning what it means to be Iñupiaq.

(Pausauraq Jana Harcharek, continued)

trained to feel and engender shame, hurt, and pain, and despite our best intentions, our children and grandchildren internalize those negative emotions.

Though we have fallen prey to colonialism and imperialistic attitudes, we did not break as a people. Through it all, we still claim identity as Iñupiat, the real people. Through it all, we remain strong and proud as a people.

It will take years for us to shatter the grip of colonization; it is not going to be easy. Global forces and pressures continue to mount. We are being faced with impending impacts on our ocean and all that we garner as gifts from the sea. This, after we have had to learn how to take care of our lands, land animals, and resources in the midst of development.

We have taken stands on several fronts. We created a governmental regime and made sure land claims were addressed to effectuate mechanisms by which to advance the Iñupiaq agenda. Our leaders have striven and continue to strive to ensure our full participation in decision-making processes that will affect our lives and our land, ocean, and resources.

As Iñupiat, we are once again starting to look from within. We are once again honoring who we are and what we believe in. We are reclaiming our past. We are regaining our right to determine what is in our children's best interests by insisting on educational reform in our schools. Imperialistic mentalities will always abound, but as a Nation we have the right to dictate the pieces that make up our educational system.

* * *

OUR INDIVIDUAL STORIES FLOW TOGETHER as we describe our separate journeys returning to Iñupiaq consciousness, which shapes our telling of the story of the Iñupiaq Learning Framework (ILF). Our stories of healing state our motivations and how each of us approaches our work in education to achieve something bigger than ourselves, to reach a place that is informed by both the past and the continuously redefined future. As Iñupiaq educators in Barrow, Alaska, we began in 2006 to develop what would become the ILF. Our community collaboration is founded upon Iñupiaq knowledge, practices, and processes that began long before we engaged in this writing project. Within our community, Elders have told our stories, and Iñupiaq educators have written about how old and new ways in education can come together (MacLean, 2010; Okakok, 2010). In this article, we share one small time frame (2006–2012) of our effort, on the North Slope of Alaska, to affirm our place and our processes for learning. Hundreds, or perhaps thousands, of questions about how best to educate our community and the children of our Iñupiaq Nation shape this inquiry. We asked: What does a successful 18-year-old Iñupiaq person look like? This became our defining question, which initiated the drawing of deep and broad strokes of the ILF and provided focus for continuous community dialogue.

We evoke Kiŋuniivut, our ancestors, and we remember their words. The work seeks to break away from an imposed educational system and away from the unbelievable pain evident in the loss of our language, cultural practices, and ways of being. The story of the ILF is a story of the process by which our community engaged in claiming our existence, our vision, and our connection with places that change with the seasons back into each and every one of our lives.

Our homeland encompasses 89,000 square miles, stretching from Tikiġaq on the westernmost point on the North Slope of Alaska to Kaktovik on the eastern coast near the Canadian border; to Anaqtuvuk Pass in the Brooks Range; Nuiqsat on the Kuukpik River; Ulġuniq and Kali on the Chukchi coast; Atqasuk on the Kuulugruaq River; and Utqiaġvik, the northernmost community on the North American continent. This area constitutes the North Slope Borough, organized as a home rule municipal government in 1972 (Andersen-Spear & Hopson, 2010, p. 1). The North Slope Borough School District (NSBSD) was formed in that same year to exercise local control over schooling. The NSBSD serves approximately 1,600 students from K3 to 12th grade

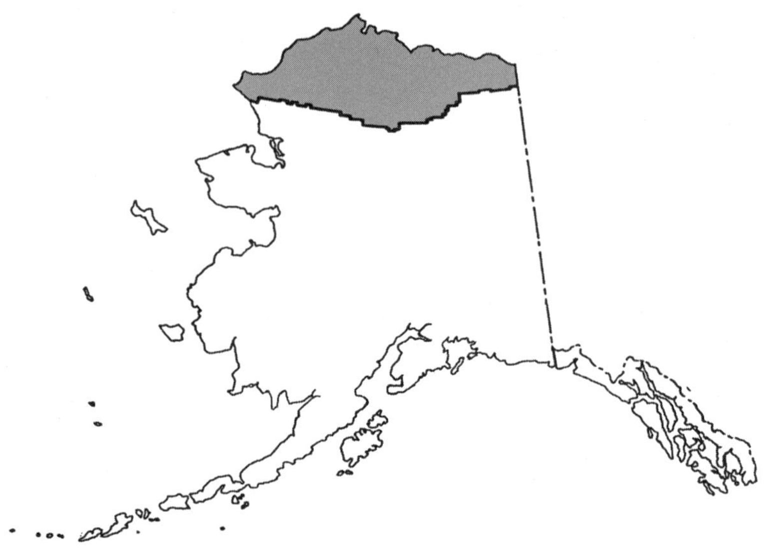

Alaska's North Slope.

(North Slope Borough School District, 2011) and employs 166 certified teachers, only one of whom is Iñupiaq.

Our students are bright and capable individuals who, too often, have been labeled and portrayed as less than the American "norm." The ILF is meant to guide instruction and expose students to curricular knowledge to help reclaim identity and determine for ourselves what constitutes "success." A primary purpose of the ILF is to effectuate change: to make the education system meaningful and culturally responsive, resulting in greater academic success for our students (Mapkuqput Iñuuniaġniġmi Iñupiaq Learning Framework, 2011).

Our work with our community sparks healing from a good place in our hearts and is informed by the risks we have taken to bring the story to you, the reader. The story is a story of healing, drawing upon the affirmation of Indigenous knowledge for the education of our Iñupiaq children.

Methodology

Kiŋuniivut, our ancestors, have told their stories, and others have written about Native educational transformation (Barnhardt & Kawagley, 2010; Battiste, 2013). We join in sharing our story, chronicling our journey to reclaim our community's right to Iñupiaq knowledge. Storytelling from memory best aligns with how we were taught to share knowledge gained, and we intentionally separate the act of "writing lessons learned" from an act of "research" in which one might set out to test a hypothesis or to seek one answer to a carefully crafted research question. Indigenous scholar Shawn Wilson (2008) articulated an approach similar to our process when he wrote:

> The use of an Indigenous research paradigm when studying Indigenous peoples requires the holistic use and transmission of information. . . . I present the information in this study in a way that is more culturally appropriate for Indigenous peoples by taking the role of storyteller rather than researcher/author. (p. 32)

Our methodology to gather knowledge and share knowledge, in order to tell this story, drew upon continuous, focused engagement with Iñupiaq Elders and community members. In these interactions, we memorized movements, places, expressions, and stories and reviewed our compiled notes, photographs, and documents.

We listened to Elders and consciously challenged ourselves to remember their words. We participated in meetings, informal and formal gatherings, ceremonies, and dances, all spaces in which learning unfolds in dynamic moments. We spent time together talking about what we experienced and learned from the community, and we attempted to make sense of our words, experiences, and knowledge. We reflected on our initial analyses, and we asked our community: What else must we ask to reach a deeper understanding of our plight, our purpose, our calling, to reveal the rich knowledge carried within our members of the Iñupiaq Nation?

Rooted in the process of writing the article are numerous acts of remembering, dialogue, and reflection. As we awaken words to mold descriptions and the story of the development of the ILF, we check our memory against notes, visual memory, and collective memory. Through the process of reflection and writing, we realize that we need to restore Iñupiaq protocols to help the ILF grow and become what we envision it to be and to ensure that it has a strong foundation and roots within the community. The act of reviving these protocols for learning and interacting with Elders, parents, and young people allows us to move forward in a good way.

When necessary, we retell the story and remember details and processes. When necessary, we return to the Iḷiññiaġnikun Apqusiuqtit, those who break the trail for learning, to check our understandings. We return to writing, adding details, building the story, and drawing upon material and visual knowledge (such as notes, agendas, recordings, and pictures). This article is a result of layering stories, memories, dialogue, debate, and resolution. The article also reflects processes of inquiry or learning protocols that are informed by Iñupiaq ways of being. Iñupiaq processes and protocols guided the development of the ILF and in turn, guided the process of writing this article and sharing knowledge.

Context: Engaging With Our Place and People

In the Arctic, there is no way one person can survive on one's own. The place where we live has molded who we are and how we relate to the world. In the wintertime, the snow sweeps a blanket over the land, demarcated in an east-west direction appearing much like a white-sands desert. The commencement of spring finds our people filled with unspoken anticipation as preparations for the spring whale hunt begin. In the summertime, the landscape bursts into colors of green, brown, and rust. The land is beautifully ripe as berries and flora cover the tundra. Flowers, grasses, and short plants shoot up as the snow melts into shallow ponds, and lakes dot the countryside. Autumn and spring transitions are more widely recognized by the loss or gain of daylight than by physical changes. As children, many of us grew up with and many of our children today are raised with a strong sense of connectedness, not only to each other but also to the land, the ocean, and the environment. Our roles as human beings are defined by the contributions we make to the greater good. We share a collective responsibility to ensure that our grandchildren and their grandchildren have a strong sense of identity and an unwavering sense of purpose in life. We are always reminded by the ceaseless changing of the seasons of the need for constant vigilance in maintaining a connectedness to all that abounds.

Speaking in general terms, Iñupiaq people are on the quiet side, more reserved and more observational than many Americans. Visitors remark that our people are warm and friendly and strongly tied to family. Family relationships and kinships are of utmost importance, as evidenced by the typical family photographic montages above one's kitchen table and living room couch. It is understood that one's support network extends to the whole community, far beyond the immediate family.

Communication is subtle and people generally speak in an indirect, nonconfrontational manner. This custom extends into our modern-day politics, business practices, and many institutions. Teasing is often used to correct behavior and show affection. Communication may be the simple act of removing your gloves to exchange a handshake and greeting or of allowing for long pauses and silence in a conversation to ensure adequate time and space for all to share, rather than speaking over someone else's thought. Frequently, these subtleties in communication have been hard for people new to the North Slope to grasp.

Of all the foundational values practiced on the North Slope, respect may be the most dynamic, the most challenging to learn, and the most interwoven into the mores of Arctic survival. Respect can mean cultivating and nurturing relationships with Elders, the natural environment, and your hunting or trading partners. The sharing of traditional foods and material possessions, naming rituals, and Iñupiaq adoption traditions are also powerful expressions of respect. The act and value of respect can often be overlooked by an untrained eye but is in fact embedded in all parts of our lives.

Spirituality permeates the homes and the hearts of most North Slope residents. While widely varied in nuance, spirituality is essential to understanding the Iñupiat. Spirituality manifests itself not only within the walls of the many churches that dot the village grids of self-contained gravel roads; an inherent practice of worship, prayer, and reverence saturates all aspects of daily life. The power of Iñupiaq song, dance, and drumming is an unparalleled phenomenon that you must witness to grasp the magnitude and depth of our environment.

Developing a basic understanding of the Iñupiaq way of life is essential for anyone new to the North Slope. In particular, educators new to the NSBSD have to be given opportunities to learn the ways in which the children with whom they will be working interact with others, in order to be better connected to their learners and thus better prepared to teach in a pedagogically sound manner.

The Epistemology: How We Have Come to Know

The reader and the teachers must understand how the Iñupiat "come to know" in order to grasp the complexity of the ILF, understand the reference points in which the knowledge is rooted, and philosophically align teaching and learning to the Iñupiaq worldview. It is vital that one understand the concept of *iñua*.

Iñua. Iñua is a spirit. The spirit that gives life, that sustains life, that creates life—from the wind and the air to the plants and the animals;

from the rivers and the oceans and the ice to the sun, the moon, and the stars.

Iñua is a shared state of awareness. It is always there, always exists, and it is a gift that we are given to experience, cultivate, and allow to move through us to restore our optimal state of being.

Iñua is a pathway, a flow of mutual respect that exists between all life forms. Iñua creates an ease of living, and we exert less energy to live as though we are flowing with the current. When we are in alignment, our efforts yield a greater outcome and experience.

Iñua is a practice. It is the actions and the inspiration of those actions of our heart, mind, spirit, and body. Iñua is the art of survival, it is infinite, and it is life. It is the practice of balance, respect, and love. Iñua is the Iñupiaq soul.

Teaching and Learning

The Iñupiaq teaching and learning continuum is whole and connected: the spirit, the learner, the teacher, and the action all enter a state of shared space and need to reach their full potential. We all depend upon one other to exist. For example, the art of sewing cannot exist without a seamstress; a larger purpose, or direction, from a more experienced source of knowledge. Our conception of learning is based on observing, internalizing, and doing. A person learns by enlightenment from a master, mentor, and practitioner who shares how to hold the new knowledge, practice the teachings, and ultimately become a master of the teaching. Learning is the conjoining of doing and doer. Acquiring the knowledge is not separated from using it, and all knowledge has a specific function. The ILF encapsulates the idea that learning is a lifelong process occurring throughout one's life in many different "venues," including at home, out on the land, in a whaling boat, and at school.

Iñupiaq Learning Framework

What is the ILF? The ILF is an individual space that allows us the opportunity to connect to our iñua and by its nature creates a collective of learners and practitioners of Iñupiaq lifeways. The ILF is a process of becoming connected to the parts of ourselves we were given as human beings: heart, mind, body, and ultimately to the spirit that connects us all. The ILF is a pathway to healing that connects us to our Iñupiaq soul, to our ancestors, and to our true selves. This knowledge we have outlined together is the stepping-stone to becoming a whole person. The ILF is the art of awareness and of being aware, as our ancestors were.

The ILF feels like a calm day on the ocean with clear skies and blue glassy water. The ILF feels like dancing to an "eskimo" drum. The ILF feels like becoming lost in a good story; transported. The ILF feels like sunshine and fresh air on *nuna*—land—that has just been rained upon. The ILF feels like a tug on your fishing line. The ILF feels like an embrace from an Elder. The ILF feels like feeding your family a wholesome meal, caught by your grandson and brought to you with a good heart. The ILF feels like looking up into the corners of a canvas tent and listening to the hiss of a Coleman stove. The ILF feels like knowing what the clouds and winds will tell you about the weather. The ILF feels like catching a caribou for the first time. The ILF feels like being able to fix your own snow machine when it breaks down. The ILF feels like a drink of the coolest, clearest glacier water. The ILF feels like watching a whale's last breath. The ILF feels like rolling laughter and joy bubbling up at the kitchen table. The ILF feels like rendered seal oil with sweet leaves. The ILF feels like a clean ice cellar. The ILF feels like the stained fingertips of a seamstress after sewing the skins for the boat. The ILF feels like a prayer at just the right moment.

The ILF gives peace, well-being, humility; it is the alignment of your personal rhythm to the Iñupiaq rhythm. It is a way to synchronize with the timeless rhythm of the seasons, of the environment, and of the work it takes to live with them. It is a way to align your actions with what you know to be your own truth, the truth that was given to you by those who raised you or by those you looked up to.

When brought to life, the ILF will be a community of people who are well; a community of people who are moving along in their healing, awareness, and ability to live a good life. The ILF will shift people to become self-determined. It will be a spiritual, intellectual, emotional, and physical energy that flows easily in each of us rather than an energy that is blocked and stagnant, creating situations of dysfunction and unhealthy behaviors. It will be an individual shift from pain to liberation, thereby creating a communal shift.

History and Context

In order to move forward, we must first know from where we came. In a speech delivered in 1976, North Slope Borough Mayor Eben Hopson expressed the desire of the community to see the Iñupiat perspective reflected in schools:

> We must now achieve "professional control" by examining the teacher and content of instruction. We must have teachers who will reflect and transmit our ideals and values. We must have Iñupiat-centered orientation in all areas of instruction. I do not want my children to learn that we were "discovered" by Columbus or Vitus Bering. I do not want to hear that we were barbaric or "uncivilized." I do not want our children to feel inferior because their language and culture are different from those of their teacher. I do not want to see school planning surveys which list hunting, fishing, whaling, or trapping as a "social" or "recreational" activity. (Hopson, 1977, n.p.)

Despite this community manifesto, the district continued to operate on a "we know what is best for you" mantra for many years. Nearly 40 years after the Iñupiat gained local control over education, the administration of the NSBSD finally acknowledged that as an institution responsible for implementing board policy, they had never gone to the people. Time had never been taken to ascertain what the people they were serving felt was important in terms of schooling. It became imperative for the district to reach out to the people.

In pursuit of building a relationship built on trust and respect, the district instituted the Iñupiaq Education Initiative. The initiative brought together Elders, students, teachers, parents—anyone who had the time and the interest—in forums designed to facilitate the articulation of their vision for school.

The process involved acknowledging our ancestors by discussing how children were raised to be responsible, contributing citizens before the arrival of schools. Community members remembered fondly how parents, grandparents, aunts, uncles, *aanas, ataatas*—everyone in the village—cared for and advised or counseled the young. The changes that occurred when schools were established were acknowledged. Many Elders regretted missing the opportunity to go to school because they were responsible for helping to sustain their families. In a profoundly meaningful exercise, participants created a net by standing in a circle and throwing a ball of yarn back and forth until each one held a part of the net. All participants who were younger than 16 were asked to let go of their part of the net and step back. The resulting discussion revealed feelings of loneliness and abandonment, as well as led to a more cohesive mutual understanding of the psychological impacts of children being shipped or flown to boarding school.

Finally, we were able to talk about where we are today and recognize the efforts of Iñupiaq leaders who saw the advantages of and pursued the formation of the North Slope Borough and the NSBSD. They had dreams for what education in our homelands should be, as do the Iñupiat of today. The people of the communities spoke and said they want the identities, the histories, the language, and the cultural practices of our people mirrored in our schools—not at the expense of academic success but rather as an integral part of schooling.

Process: Breaking the Trail for Learning

Among other responsibilities, the Iñupiaq Education Department of the NSBSD is charged with providing professional development to teachers who, quite often, have a limited understanding of how our Iñupiaq children think, what can be intellectually stimulating for them, and what best practices look like for teaching, given our environment. After some years of applying a one-shot-a-year approach wherein we (the authors) traveled to each site and provided "cultural" inservices, we became more cognizant that what was missing was a road map that clearly spelled out the expectations of the community and supported the mission of the district. The mission stated in part: "Learning in our schools is rooted in the values, history and language of the Iñupiat" (North Slope Borough School District Board, 2010). Teachers were equipped with the Alaska State Content and Performance Standards with accompanying Grade Level Expectations but lacked the cultural component. This awareness led to dialogue about how we needed to define what we want our children to learn and be proficient in by the time they graduate.

We invited representatives from the three major North Slope dialectal groups to join what we initially called the Iñupiaq Cultural Advisory Committee. The questions posed to the group were designed to elicit a definition of what a well-grounded, well-educated young Iñupiaq person looks like today. During the analysis of their initial input, it became clear that the group was serving in a capacity far more encompassing than we had originally envisioned. They were guiding our collective thought processes to determine the way in which learning would be directed in the district. To honor and acknowledge their refined purpose, the group was renamed Iḷiññiaġnikun Apqusiuqtit, "people who break the trail for learning." Clearly, they endeavored to break the trail for curriculum reform in the district.

Over the course of a year, we held four gatherings. At the first gathering, we built a foundation and came to a common understanding of our collective purpose. During the second and third gatherings, we created a framework of history, skills, knowledge, stories, and values. At the final gathering, we reviewed the material outcomes of our work, specifically, the depiction of the ILF. In each meeting, we began our journey together in prayer, and we held the space to heal together. Each person was heard, made contributions, and became inspired as we envisioned the possibilities of this undertaking. We used the space as an opportunity to ground ourselves in the larger purpose and the reasons we were gathered together, to connect with the spirit from which our ancestral knowledge comes, and to prepare the group for the intense work that was to come in subsequent gatherings. Notably, the dynamic of holding the space in Iñupiaq nurtured our collective iñua and encouraged a deep level of sharing, healing, learning, and opening to the inspiration of this profound Iñupiaq knowledge in what we would come to know as the Iñupiaq Learning Framework.

Mapkuqput Iñuuniaġniġmi

When asked to describe her artistic rendering of the list of Iñupiaq knowledge and skills, Iñupiaq artist Rainey Nasuġraq Hopson stated:

> The life of an Iñupiaq can be characterized by how one interacts with the world and all of its components. The Iñupiaq World consists of four major realms: The Environment, the Community, History and Individual—pieces in the blanket that are needed to carry and elevate an individual to success. Surrounding the blanket are the people making this happen, the community at large and our ancestors. There are eight pairs of people representing the eight villages of the North Slope. They are all looking upward as they raise their children to the heights of achievement. The attributes needed to attain those heights are all intertwining pieces on the blanket. The red stitching found throughout the blanket represents our Iñupiaq Language, as it is the element that ties and binds all of these concepts and qualities together. (personal communication, March 10, 2010)

Nasuġraq adeptly captured the essence of our worldview in a powerful and moving image, which is based on the *mapkuq*, the blanket used in the celebration of a successful whaling season.

The Environmental Realm entails our connection to the environment and all that is contained within it, including the air we breathe. Our surroundings provide for the life we are able to live. The tools and the technology that are crafted from the land and from the animals of

Mapkuqput Innuuniaġniġmi—the blanket of life. Copyright North Slope Borough School District (2010).

our land and waters reflect a long-standing relationship we have maintained over countless generations. We are dependent on our environment and as such, must engender an understanding of and a respect for this vital relationship in our descendants. The fish symbolizes food preparation and care; the arrow represents hunting and survival; the bone needle—the art of sewing; the open hand—tools, both modern and old; the stem and the leaf—healing and medicine practices; and the mountain and the sea—our knowledge of and care for our sacred ecosystems.

The Community Realm involves thoughts and practices embodied by the proverb, "It takes a village to raise a child." This proverb has applied to the Iñupiat since time immemorial. Our people have practiced ancient rites of passage, efficacious rituals, and transformative ceremonies. Our society has a complex web of relations from which teachings about life emanate. Living in harmony requires mutual respect, understanding, and communication. These community practices are essential for our children's emotional, intellectual, physical, and spiritual well-being. The two Elders are representative of our devotion to and respect for them; the raised whale bones—ceremonies and celebrations; the dancer—song and dance; the storyteller and the audience—storytelling and Iñupiaq lore; the mask—arts; the parent and the child—parenting; the skin ball—games and competition; and the family—our web of relationships.

The Historical Realm is indicative of how in the time continuum of the Iñupiat, we are one generation held accountable to the next. It is our responsibility to keep our knowledge alive, just as those who came before us took it upon themselves to learn the stories and pass them on. The stories we tell and our own understandings will one day become legends, and our descendants will speak of us as we speak of those who came before us. For our children to have an Iñupiaq identity, it is essential for us to ground them in this way. We must provide them with a broad historical scope, exceptionally rich in detail. The timeline with a storyteller and an audience represents our Unipkaat, Quliaqtuat, and Uqaluktuat, which are our stories; the timeline with a map of the North Slope speaks to our history; and the timeline with a globe acknowledges our more recent history concomitant with our place in the world.

The Individual Realm recognizes that as Iñupiat, we are lifelong learners. We all have roles in our families and communities. Some individuals are born hunters, dancers, or seamstresses. Some have the gift of song or storytelling. Others dedicate their lives to history, being a good parent, or perhaps doing well in business or the arts. We must prepare our future generations for whatever paths they choose to walk in their lifetimes. Our idea of "self" is depicted in the center of the image. The caribou antler communicates balance and navigating effectively amidst myriad cultural domains; the leader—leadership skills; the *ulu*—women's roles; the rising sun—values and beliefs; the knife—men's roles; the crescent moon—the importance and significance of names in Iñupiaq society; and the dotted path in the center is indicative of the Iñupiaq life cycle.

Ownership of the ILF is time intensive. Allowing for space in our lives to create and acquire the knowledge and the skills that would be defined as Iñupiaq is key to success. This project began in response to the call of our Elders, who wanted to see their children and grandchildren live successful lives and wished for them to see this world as Iñupiat. Their example of sharing knowledge set the tone for the rest of the song that we are creating. When we think of ownership, let us remember their words, their spirits, their laughter, their wisdom, and their compassion. Let us be inspired by their actions and by the care they give to us.

The ILF is dynamic because it began, is nourished by, and came to exist from a collective of voices. It honors specialized knowledge that is Iñupiaq. Ownership is not something to achieve; it is something that catalyzes and sustains the work itself. It is the oxygen the ILF needs to survive. Without continued ownership, it will cease to exist. The ILF is the foundation and must be central to all activities, all developments, and all endeavors connected to this work.

There are two significant challenges in the implementation of the ILF. The first is training teachers to become the learners of the lifeways of the Iñupiat. Most are not from the North Slope and lack the knowledge base to make appropriate academic connections to the ILF. The second is collaborating with community members to join in this shared responsibility. Community members need to become teachers of teachers. They need to be the medium through which teachers become educated. Then collectively, we all become the transmitters of Iñupiaq knowledge.

Our district holds the expectation that teachers engage in developing strong instructional practices that are guided by the ILF, which holds our community's expectations about what Iñupiaq youth should experience in their schooling. Looking backward as the district moves into the third year of its curriculum alignment, integration, and mapping effort, we have pondered and pored over the obstacles we have faced, including the discomfort teachers report about implementing the ILF. They feel it is "not their place to teach the culture." This dilemma has required a rethinking of the approach we had been using in the inservicing of teachers. Our goal has become one of familiarizing teachers with the ILF and bringing about a consequential comfort level in its application. Teachers can now use this tool to honor the legacy of the children they serve. As a result, the long-term expectation is that our children, who will no longer be expected to leave their identity as Iñupiat outside the door when they come to school, will come to know that teaching is an honorable profession and become teachers themselves.

Conclusion and Significance: Returning to the Source, and the ILF Legacy

Iñuguġniq is a concept that denotes the spirit and essence of one's experiences in the journey of becoming a whole human being; it translates to "the process of becoming a human being." We have the power to determine for ourselves what is important for our children to learn. It is our responsibility. We have a place in the world the same as in time immemorial, and the lenses through which we view and interpret the world are inimitable. What greater gift is there than the gift of knowledge as seen through our perspective? With the ILF serving as the foundation upon which the school district operates, delivers instruction, and articulates the curriculum, we are coming full circle. We are returning to the way it once was, albeit in a modern, contemporary context. We are reawakening to the constant presence of our ancestors and through the work of the ILF, consciously honoring them. In the same way our ancestors drew upon their strengths to ensure continued survival, we too must have the stamina, resilience, endurance, and wherewithal to ensure a future bright with hope, love, and honor for our future generations.

We have always believed that as a people, we have the right to determine content and instructional delivery methodologies. We also must reclaim the timeless pedagogical strategies of our ancestors and incorporate those into our mindset. We must be committed to shifting ideology, a shift that embraces all that the ILF stands for, a shift that translates to a standard district operating ethic. For the sake of our ancestors and those who are to follow, we can and will rise to the occasion and realize the vision of our Elders to make our schools genuinely reflective of our people.

As we set out to reflect and tell this story for the first time in Colorado, a cold front swept through the middle of spring, bringing snow. Catching most by surprise, this presence was a sure sign that our ancestors were with us, guiding us to the realizations needed to explain the complexities of the ILF. Their presence was emblematic of the power of this work. Our connection to the ancestors has been strong and consistent throughout the creation of the ILF. As more people open themselves to the possibilities the ILF can offer, their response is equally powerful; it is as though one is in the presence of an ancestor, and there is a moment of mutual recognition as the person recognizes his or her spirit in the ILF, and the ILF recognizes the spirit of the person. In this sacred space, the powerful process of transformation begins.

We have learned that we are not separate from this knowledge; it is a part of us. There is not one pathway to learning, but many. All of our stories of learning are precious and important. The ways in which we live healthy, balanced, positive lives are important. To begin small practices of learning creates healing, growth, and opportunity for further and deeper learning. It is a choice to learn Iñupiaq lifeways—it is a choice you make every day. It is both the gift you are given and it is the gift you give. Our lifeways are intelligent, savvy, beautiful, and powerful: They teach us so that we may experience life as an Iñupiaq.

As we reflect on how we achieved this work together, we are acutely aware of times when it does not feel authentic, times when iñua is missing, and times when we are not involving people in a real way or allowing the connections to flourish. It is a tangible feeling and creates situations of stress and imbalance. There have been countless days, months, and years when we have had to pause, reflect, and readjust to ensure that we are involving community people; that we are opening spaces for them to contribute in a meaningful way and giving back to them as much as they are giving to us.

We are at an interesting moment in the growth of the ILF. So much has been done and yet so much more remains to be done. An element of trust remains unspoken in the creation of the ILF; neither the facilitators nor the community knows where and how the changes will occur or how this project will shift and grow and change. We do not know what it will grow up to be. All we can do is provide it a safe place to be nurtured and explore the infinite possibilities that lie ahead. All we can do is provide safe spaces for the spirit, the people, and the time to come together and grow.

When we heal and grow together, we add our voices to the song our Elders inspired; we become acknowledged and a part of something bigger. We embody the full potential of our special and unique place in the continuum of our ancestors. We become a part of the bonds of knowledge, language, and values that stretch back to the beginning of time. We have both the luxury and the necessity to discover what it means to be Iñupiaq in 2012. In this opportunity, we can see that perhaps this point we are at in the creation of the ILF also reflects the larger schema of Iñupiaq existence. In no other point in our history has this rare occasion presented itself. We have always been busy with the work it takes to survive in the Arctic, and now, precisely because of the abundant amounts of time we have because of modern technologies, we can reflect on where we are as a people and create ways to flourish in the future. This opportunity is a gift, if we choose to see it that way. Let us live up to this opportunity and move forward together. Let this be the story of the Iñupiaq Learning Framework. Let this be our story of healing.

Pausauraq Jana Harcharek *(Iñupiaq) is Director of Iñupiaq Education at the North Slope Borough School District in Barrow, Alaska.*

Cathy Tagnak Rexford *(Iñupiaq) is a recent graduate of the Joint MFA Creative Writing and Theatre Program at the University of British Columbia.*

ACKNOWLEDGMENTS

Quyanaqpak to the members of Iḷiññiaġnikun Apqusiuqtit: Ugiaqtaq Wesley Aiken, Napaaqtuq Mario Gamboa, Qaiyaan Harcharek, Aanauraq Lillian Lane Johnson, Aŋutuqsana Rex Okakok, Kisautaq Leona Okakok, Kakianaaq Molly Pederson, Iyaaq Rossman Peetook, and Sisualik Rachel Riley. They truly blazed the trail for learning. Quyanapiallak also to Kuutuuq Fannie Akpik, who has been with us all the way. Our deepest and most heartfelt gratitude for Qannik Tarajean Yazzie-Mintz, whose guidance was infused with iñua from the beginning to the end, which really, is the beginning of a new chapter.

REFERENCES

Andersen-Spear, D., & Hopson, E. (2010). Alaska Native education: Past, present, and future. In R. Barnhardt & A. O. Kawagley (Eds.), *Alaska Native education: Views from within* (pp. 1–6). Fairbanks: Alaska Native Knowledge Network.

Barnhardt, R., & Kawagley, A. O. (Eds.). (2010). *Alaska Native education: Views from within.* Fairbanks: Alaska Native Knowledge Network.

Battiste, M. (2013). *Decolonizing education: Nourishing the learning spirit.* Saskatoon, Canada: Purich.

Hopson, E. (1977). *Iñupiaq education.* Retrieved from http://www.alaskool.org/native_ed/historicdocs/people/inup_edu.html

MacLean, E. A. (2010). Culture and change for Iñupiat and Yup'ik people of Alaska. In R. Barnhardt & A. O. Kawagley (Eds.), *Alaska Native education: Views from within* (pp. 41–58). Fairbanks: Alaska Native Knowledge Network.

Mapkuqput Iñuuniaġniġmi Iñupiaq Learning Framework. (2011). *Mapkuqput Iñuuniaġniġmi: Iñupiaq Learning Framework.* Barrow, AK: North Slope Borough School District.

North Slope Borough School District Board. (2010). *NSBSD board strategic plan, 2010–2015.* Barrow, AK: North Slope Borough School District.

North Slope Borough School District. (2011). *Report card to the public: School year 2011–2012.* Barrow, AK: North Slope Borough School District.

Okakok, L. (2010). Serving the purpose of education. In R. Barnhardt & A. O. Kawagley (Eds.), *Alaska Native education: Views from within* (pp. 99–124). Fairbanks: Alaska Native Knowledge Network.

Wilson, S. (2008). *Research is ceremony: Indigenous research methods.* Halifax, Nova Scotia, Canada: Fernwood.

Designing Pedagogies for Indigenous Science Education: Finding Our Way to Storywork

ANANDA MARIN and MEGAN BANG

This article explores teachers' sense-making in teaching science. The literature on nonmajority teachers' experiences in designing and planning for instruction is limited. Examinations of teachers' understandings of science teaching and learning in the context of educational reform have failed to look closely at teachers as designers of community-based science-learning environments. We analyze the sense-making that occurred when American Indian teachers met in an informal learning environment to design and implement science curricula. Findings reveal that teachers engaged with community-based stories while designing curricula and framed stories in terms of lesson launches or instructional beginnings (Jackson, Garrison, Wilson, Gibbons, & Shahan, 2013). Drawing on the work of Jo-ann Archibald (2008), we view this process as akin to "storywork" and suggest that teacher design meetings serve as a critical site of sense-making where teachers can build shared knowledge of science content and design pedagogies that are "culturally sustaining and revitalizing" (McCarty & Lee, 2014).

EPISTEMOLOGICAL ORIENTATIONS are crucial to science learning and teaching (American Association for the Advancement of Science/Project 2061, 1993). They influence the scope of activities considered in science education and the form that science practices take as well as participation in practices in learning environments (Bang & Medin, 2010; Deloria, 1979, 1997). By epistemological orientations, we mean basic notions about knowledge, knowledge construction, knowledge dissemination, and dispositions to use particular knowledge forms. Indigenous scholars have called attention to the ever-present need to understand the places where curricula are enacted and how they stand in relation to and with Indigenous epistemologies (Deloria & Wildcat, 2001; Kawagley, 1995; Richardson, 2011). As Cajete (2005) writes:

> There is no word for *epistemology* in any American Indian language. However, there is certainly a body of understandings that can be said to

> include what this branch of Western philosophy would explore as the origins, nature, and methods of coming to know a way of life. . . . American Indian education historically occurred in a holistic social context that developed a sense of the importance of each individual as a contributing member of the social group. Essentially, tribal education worked as a cultural and life-sustaining process. It was a process of education that unfolded through reciprocal relationships between one's social group and the natural world. (pp. 69–70)

Importantly, Cajete calls attention to reciprocal relationships and the role of the natural world in tribal education and the development of identities. The creative act of listening to and telling stories and understanding oneself intellectually, spiritually, emotionally, and physically in relation to relatives (human, plant, and animal), nature, and land are central to science education (Archibald, 2008; Cajete, 2000).

In this article, we reflect on our experiences as teacher-researchers within a community-based design research project that increased participation and interest in science by implementing science lessons based around the big idea of living in relationships (see Bang, Medin, Washinawatok, & Chapman, 2010). We suggest that developing pedagogical expertise for science teaching that is "culturally sustaining and revitalizing" (McCarty & Lee, 2014) requires a creative space in community contexts where teachers can: (1) engage in joint sense-making about the dynamic tensions and generativities between Native science and Western science, (2) learn to see science as a storytelling activity, and (3) develop their capacity to listen to and tell stories for the purposes of science teaching and learning. In this article, we focus on moments of teachers' pedagogical theorizing in order to illustrate the evolving role of community-based stories in teachers' planning of science-related activities.

Motivation

Broadening participation and success in the sciences among Indigenous youth requires that we attend to community-based ways of knowing and doing (Aikenhead, 1997; Bang et al., 2010; Barnhardt & Kawagley, 2005; Cajete, 2000; Kawagley, 1995; Nelson-Barber & Estrin, 1995). Considerable effort has been directed toward creating curricula and learning environments that mobilize students' community-based repertoires and position students to acquire privileged scientific literacies (Aikenhead, 1997; Barnhardt & Kawagley, 2005; Nelson-Barber &

Estrin, 1995). In addition, education researchers have taken up students' navigation between multiple ways of knowing and teachers' roles in supporting students' navigation—what is often called learning in *hybrid* or *third* spaces (Gutierrez, Baquedano-Lopez, & Tejeda, 1999; Lee, 2001; Moll, Amanti, Neff, & Gonzalez, 1992; Nasir, Rosebery, Warren, & Lee, 2006; Rosebery, Warren, & Conant, 1992; Warren, Ballenger, Ogonowski, Rosebery, & Hudicourt-Barnes, 2001). However, there has been less work on how Indigenous teachers navigate multiple epistemologies and understand the cultural nature of their own practice (Brayboy & Maughan, 2009; Maaka, Au, Lefcourt, & Bogac, 2001; Yazzie-Mintz, 2007).

The challenge for teacher educators and educational researchers is to support the development of Indigenous teachers' identity and their ability to design hybrid spaces that restore teaching and learning to an intellectual and community development activity. Specifically, we are concerned with better understanding how teachers work their community-based ways of knowing to understand science content (both Western and Indigenous) and develop culturally sustaining and revitalizing pedagogies. Reflecting on our own experiences developing and implementing science-learning environments, we became interested in how we, as designers, researchers, and teachers, navigated community-based ways of knowing and Western scientific ways of knowing to develop shared epistemological frames, effective pedagogies, and practice.

Research Context

The present work has evolved from our participation in a research project with one of the oldest and largest urban Indian centers in the country. The community center is a primary cultural resource for Native Americans residing in the area. The project focused on supporting students' navigation between Native ways of knowing, or Indigenous knowledge systems, and Western scientific ways of knowing. Utilizing community-based design research methods, a primary project goal was to improve science learning and school achievement for Native American middle school students. The project also examined the impact of ecological knowledge organization and relational epistemologies on cognition.

Reconfiguring Power and Self-Determination Through Design Research

Indigenous scholars have suggested that self-determination requires the reclaiming, uncovering, and reinventing of our theoretical understandings and pedagogical best practices (e.g., Bang, 2008; Battiste, 2002; Smith et al., 2002; Tippeconnic, 1999). This project retooled design research with the intention of affording Indigenous youth, adults, and caregivers the autonomy to work through the intergenerational trauma that has defined our experiences with formal education and to wrestle with the complexities of educational self-determination (Duran, Duran, & Yellow Horse Brave Heart, 1998; Tippeconnic, 1999; Tuck, 2009). We term this methodology *community-based design research* (CBDR) (see Bang et al., 2010). Design research can be defined as a metamethodology with the goal of designing learning environments, progressively refining new teaching strategies, and articulating learning theories (Brown, 1992; Collins, Joseph, & Bielaczyc, 2004; Design Based Research Collaborative, 2003). In typical design projects, the decision makers or designers are not drawn from students' communities. As an initial step in retooling design research, we engaged a broad range of community members from the community center in the design and enactment of learning activities. The design team included elders, parents, community content experts, content professionals, other interested adult community members, and youth. We also asked a number of designers to take on the role of teacher or facilitator. The intent was to support community members in reclaiming the classroom level of teaching and learning for Indigenous children (Smith, 1999).

A central component of CBDR as we enacted it included teacher design meetings. During the first 2 years of the project, the majority of work was completed in biweekly community designer meetings in which the learning goals and architecture of the program were constructed. The team developed and implemented curricular units that were built around the big idea of living in relationships and emphasized relationships to place (Bang et al., 2010). Units were implemented over the summer in a 2-week pilot study. Teachers engaged in two additional iterations of designing a program for summer sessions. In the fourth round of design, the program was integrated into the afterschool program at the community center, and teachers delivered lessons on weeknights, in the summer, and on Saturday family days on a biweekly basis at a local forest preserve.

Teacher design meetings became a regular feature of the project after the first 2 to 3 years and were attended by teachers and the project coordinator. These meetings afforded teachers opportunities to collectively design science lessons from community-based ways of knowing rather than plan lessons from a delegated curriculum. During the meetings, teachers talked about a range of issues, from the sequencing of activities, to methods for facilitating conversations about the nature of science, to understanding soil testing and building relationships with plants. It is important to note that between design meetings, teachers implemented lessons at the community center and in local forest preserves. The present analysis emerged from a broader analysis of teacher design meetings. Moving forward, we use the term *teacher design meetings* or *design meetings* to index the planning space.

Conceptual Framework

Teacher design meetings parallel what are also known as *teacher planning meetings* (Rosebery, 2005; Zembal-Saul, Blumenfeld, & Krajcik, 2000). Research on teacher learning points to planning meetings as a potential support for teachers as they develop content expertise over time (Rosebery, 2005; Zembal-Saul et al., 2000). Planning meetings assist teachers in anticipating problems, transforming knowledge, and developing lessons (Zembal-Saul et al., 2000). Meetings are often situated in teachers' life experiences and play an important role in the instructional cycle by providing an imaginative space where teachers can think about students' experiences and prior knowledge (Rosebery, 2005). Despite this rich literature on teacher lesson planning, Davis, Petish, and Smithey (2006) note that there is limited research on how teachers engage in long-term planning for instruction. Furthermore, although science instruction in out-of-school settings has been taken up (see National Research Council, 2009, 2012), teacher planning for instruction in such settings is rarely addressed or analyzed. The analysis presented in this paper examines Indigenous teachers' engagement in the design of out-of-school science learning environments across time. We specifically take up how we, along with our colleagues, came to see instructional beginnings in relation to storywork.

Engaging With Community Stories

In *Indigenous Storywork,* Archibald (2008) discusses the importance of understanding cultural teachings (i.e., principles and practices) and their connection to stories. She details the process of *storywork* or "learning about the nature of indigenous stories and . . . their application to education" (p. 3). As Archibald explains, the processes of colonization and schooling had an impact on Indigenous peoples' relationship to oral traditions and their "ability to make story meaning in a traditional way" (p. 14). Using traditional or community-based stories in formal learning environments requires continuous work with community members and elders. The relationship between learners and stories is reciprocal in nature and akin to being on a journey.

In this article, we explore conceptual dynamics among Native teachers during design meetings. In particular, we discuss the ways in which teachers engaged with community stories (see also Archibald, 2008; Cajete, 2000; Leonard, 2008) as they made sense of science content and developed pedagogical strategies. We take the perspective that scholars before us have articulated, namely, that stories and storytelling are central to science practices of explaining and theory building (see, for example, Ochs, Taylor, Rudolph, & Smith, 1992). For example, scholars have suggested that stories explain phenomena in the natural world and metaphorically describe ecological relationships (Aikenhead, 1997; Kawagley, 1995). Cajete (2000) describes Native science as "essentially a story, an explanation of the how and why of the things of nature and the nature of things" (p. 13). Cajete explains that stories hold information about relationships and the creative process or coming to know (i.e., knowledge production). We explore how teachers came to see stories as an important entry point for science instruction.

Lesson Launches and Storytelling

Some scholars have noted the importance of task setup for shaping learning opportunities (Jackson et al., 2013; Stein, Grover, & Henningsen, 1996). In evolving conceptions of ambitious instruction, a typical lesson sequence often follows an introduction of a complex task, followed by students working on solving the task, a whole class discussion, and sharing of work (Stein, Engle, Smith, & Hughes, 2008; Van de Walle, Folk, Karp, & Bay-Williams, 2010). Research has demonstrated that the quality and rigor of the setup or lesson launch significantly predicts the quality of the cognitive demand throughout the course of instruction, has an impact on student engagement, and finally shapes opportunities for learning in the concluding whole class discussion (Jackson et al., 2013). Features of quality launches include eliciting students' ideas and experiences and orchestrating discussion of those experiences in relationship to core disciplinary ideas (Jackson et al., 2013; Stein et al., 2008).

A teacher's epistemological frame, or his or her expectations about ways of knowing and the forms that knowledge may take, not only influences what he or she notices about students' thinking but also the teacher's development of instructional tasks (Elby & Hammer, 2010). We propose that CBDR is one domain in which teachers can gain experience with *storywork* and develop curricula from community-based ways of knowing. Informed by findings on ambitious curricula, we specifically focus on teacher talk about the launch of instruction or what we think of as instructional beginnings. We attend to moments when stories were taken up as a way to introduce science content or work through a complex science concept. We also examine the ways in which talk about stories revealed teachers' epistemological frames and shifted pedagogical theorizing toward "cultural and life-sustaining processes" (Cajete, 2005). We ask: How do teachers frame stories and storytelling in relation to science knowledge, teaching, and learning?

Methods

Teacher design meetings lasted from 1 to 3 hours. The meetings were regularly recorded and transcribed, and the data corpus consisted of 47 transcripts. We analyzed these transcripts in order to better understand teacher sense-making as well as the resources teachers drew upon when developing lesson plans and pedagogical tools. Using the transcripts, we charted themes that emerged during these meetings. This yielded six main domains of talk, including: (1) science content, (2) scaffolds and navigating, (3) stories, (4) models and representations, (5) big ideas and main topics, and (6) relationships to place. This thematic analysis highlighted the role of stories in teachers' meaning making. From these findings, we began to systematically explore the role of stories in teachers' knowledge construction and pedagogical theorizing. In this article, we present an analysis of three teacher design meetings which took place across a 5-month period. We selected these meetings for further analysis because teachers explicitly explored stories and solidified storytelling as a way to launch lessons as a core practice. We trace the evolution of teachers' understanding and engagement with stories across these meetings. Before presenting our analysis, we share information about the teachers' backgrounds.

Teacher Backgrounds

Eight community members served as teachers, and we focus on transcripts across a period of time when four of those teachers and one of the lead project principal investigators regularly participated in design and implementation. All of the teachers served as mentors and tutors in afterschool programs at the community center; however, not all of our teachers were degreed or certified. The choice was made to "grow our own" (see also http://growyourownteachers.org) science teachers rather than to recruit certified science teachers for our project. The group decided that having American Indian teachers provided the most fertile beginning point to build from and allowed our youth to see us engaging with expertise from within the community. Below, we provide brief sketches of the teachers as well as the project coordinator:

- Tyler. Tyler is Little Shell Band Chippewa Cree and Serbian. Tyler holds a PhD in cultural anthropology and identifies as an ethnobotanist. He was involved in the planning and implementation of the community center's medicinal garden and coordinates garden activities.
- Max. Max is Lakota, Italian, and German. He worked at the community center for 7 years, and his positions included volunteer, youth worker, youth program coordinator, professional development coordinator, research assistant, and community teacher. He holds a bachelor's degree in the social sciences, a master of arts in teaching, and is certified as a secondary history teacher.
- Joe. Joe is Navajo and Anishinabe. He has a bachelor's degree in environmental science and professional work experience related to his degree. He has served as an academic advisor at a state university in a Native American support program. He will be earning a master's degree in restoration ecology in December 2015.
- Ananda Marin. I am of Choctaw, African American, and European American descent. My experience in education includes developing youth programming, working at a children's museum, serving as a community college administrator, and teaching in community-based and community college settings. Shortly after joining this project, I entered a graduate program in learning sciences and earned the doctorate in December 2013.
- Megan Bang. I am of Anishinabe and Italian descent. I hold a doctorate in learning sciences and have experience developing

programs and teaching in preschool, middle school, high school, GED, higher education, and museum settings. In addition, I served as director of education at the community center for 12 years. I have professional experience coordinating, implementing, and researching professional development with teachers, and I am one of the project's principal investigators.

In the next section, we share discourse from two teacher design meetings to explore teachers' theorizing with stories while planning for classroom-level events. We frame the meetings in terms of pedagogical questions and decisions related to stories. For each meeting, we provide the design context, share teacher discourse that is specifically related to stories, and summarize how teachers conceptualized stories in relation to science teaching.

Launching Science Instruction With Stories

Design Event One: "Was There Any Storytelling Before . . . We Get Into the Lesson Plan?"

Design Context. Max, Tyler, and Joe attended this meeting in early fall 2008. Two questions were posed early on, which shaped the conversation. Max asked a question about stratigraphy, and Joe asked about stories. Max's question preceded Joe's and laid the groundwork for a discussion about stories in service of understanding science concepts such as stratigraphy:

MAX: So the stratigraphy, would that also explain the different layers of rock when we are talking about water filtering? Would that be the term we would use to wrap the kid's head around the different layers? Isn't that stratigraphy?

JOE: Yes, stratigraphy is the process of layering between different types of elements, sand or different types of chemicals, so when they layer, it depends on where they are at in their environment. The most obvious one is in the ocean because a lot of our earth has been under water. A lot of our past, of our earth history. So depending on the situation like the temperature or the gas in the air and so on. You have the different banding of different types of rocks.

MAX: So I could see that stratigraphy as being a vocabulary word or some word that we want to push on the first day when they are actually building it and physically putting in the different layers and then have a "what is porosity?" be something that we talk about on the second when we are putting water into the different models.

JOE: This could fall in line with geological time, too. We can use that as a lesson plan. Geological time and we could make a model for that also. All we need is, do you remember how our filter settled? We have a bottom of some type of container. Put some sand in the water and let it settle down until it is flat. Put a different type or size in there, maybe just move it around but you get the idea of the earth moving around under the surface. Say for example we have a bowl, and we let the bowl settle until it is flat like this and then after it settles it would be 10 minutes or so, we'll tilt it as if representing moving tectonic plates. We'll put another layer of different colored sand and let that settle. The idea is that you get different layers.

MAX: Absolutely. I could see that being a lesson that would happen before we even built any of the models that we are actually, before we did the water filtering model or the water table model because that model that you just talked about just touched on the explanation of stratigraphy.

In posing his question, Max is attempting to make sense of a scientific concept, stratigraphy, and how it applies to a potential curricular activity. In addition, he is curious about how students may understand the concept. In answer to Max's question, Joe provides a geological and historical perspective, and Max moves the group along to think about the development of a lesson plan.

This exchange between Max and Joe highlights two emergent patterns: (1) the important role variable expertise plays in teacher planning and (2) the development of shared pedagogical stances. Max, who has 5 years of experience working with students, is navigating between his own understandings of earth science concepts, his goal of promoting conceptual understanding, and his beliefs about learning by doing. His interest is centered on the concept of stratigraphy and the power the concept might have as an explanatory tool. He relies on Joe's expertise in earth science to verify and develop his own knowledge of stratigraphy. Joe, who has educational and practical experience in earth science, shares his knowledge of scientific concepts in the role of expert, but he also reframes the conversation by moving away from taxonomic descriptions and situating stratigraphy in a historical context. Joe's initial reframing of stratigraphy to include a historical perspective opens the space to discuss relationships to place, as well as representations of knowledge and forms of knowledge transmission (i.e., traditional stories).

Teacher Discourse About Stories. Joe introduces stories as a way to launch science lessons when he asks:

> JOE: In past classes or lessons, was there any storytelling before, like a quick 3-minute storytelling before we get into the lesson plan?

The transition from stratigraphy and models to storytelling suggests that this group of teachers root their understanding of science in their sociocultural histories and social context. Here, Joe's utterance can be interpreted as an epistemological framing of storytelling as a resource and a question about the role of stories in launching science lessons. However, we note that Joe's approach may be underestimating the impact of storytelling when used to launch lessons. Additionally, Joe positions storytelling as outside the lesson plan, indicating that he may see science lessons and storytelling as distinct practices. Max responds to Joe's question by detailing the ways in which stories have been used in previous lessons. He explains that stories have not been consistently told but that elders have been invited to share stories about people's relationships with animals and plants. By way of example, he describes how one elder visited over the summer and shared a story about a coyote wandering around downtown (in the city where this project occurred) and another story about a mountain lion that decided to make a nature trail its home. Joe then says:

> JOE: What I am curious about or what would be interesting for me is, find a story, doesn't matter which tribe, a story about how areas are formed. . . . So we can have a quick 5-minute story which will hopefully settle them down a little bit. We'll have an idea of what was thought and how that relates to the science part of it and how we can connect the two. That opens up a great big can of worms of discussion of why they believe it or why they don't believe it.

In this utterance, Joe is still attending to the time of the telling, but he also conceptualizes stories as explanations of how things come to be and explicitly starts to frame stories in relation to Western science (i.e., "relates to the science part of it and how we can connect the two"). However, he knows this relationship is complicated and potentially "opens up a great big can of worms." This in turn introduces another element of Joe's thinking about the role of stories in teaching: He believes that stories will capture children's attention and interest and will "settle [the students] down." The teachers then discuss various stories about place and geological formations that are familiar to each of them. They discuss the ways that stories can be used in service of science. Joe suggests that they use stories to think about relationships, and Max describes stories as "a great way to outline specific inquiries into why this erosion is happening faster." Joe then raises a concern:

> JOE: One flag for me would be as far as stories are concerned, we have some stories that can't just be thrown out and told so we need to be respectful in that regard. It would be interesting also to give the kids a task to find a story that involves a mountain or the building of a river.

This utterance makes evident an important shift in Joe's thinking about stories. Previously, Joe thought about using stories to introduce science. Here, Joe has started to shift his perspective on stories from story as telling to story as a knowledge site embedded within community protocols. He has also shifted to think about how youth might take a more active role in engaging with stories. Although this shift is subtle, we suggest that this utterance marked a turn in the teachers' sensemaking. Previously, stories were sitting outside the lesson plan; after this discussion the teachers began to weave stories into their sensemaking in more fluid ways.

Following this turn, the teachers talk about culturally significant mountain ranges and the science of volcanoes. They discuss human-nature relationships and the ways in which human activity has had an impact on mountain ranges. Tyler reflects on the everyday stories elders have shared with him and considers the interrelationships between the disappearance of natural entities (such as rocks, mountain ranges, etc.) and the loss of cultural knowledge. The teachers continue to discuss the causes and effects of erosion and make links to possible future lessons on policy, sacred sites, and land rights. We suggest that the expansion to policy, sacred sites, and land rights is connected to the shift in how stories were being taken up—that is, the learning objectives shifted from the teaching of Western science to the teaching of Indigenous science, which incorporates all of these aspects. Joe expands on his earlier comment about being respectful when telling stories, and he expresses concern about the use of knowledge, whether or not it is in the public domain, and the importance of asking permission to share certain knowledge.

Summary. This design meeting afforded teachers a space to navigate between Western and Indigenous forms of science. The two questions presented in this meeting ("Isn't that stratigraphy?" and "Was there any storytelling before?") were taken up in different ways, but both shaped the ensuing conversation and teacher sense-making. Teachers drew on their knowledge in the scientific domain and from their everyday experiences, including the urban intertribal context, and the collective knowledge that is held and shared in traditional American Indian stories. Importantly, this meeting exemplifies how stances toward stories shifted. During this design event, teachers increasingly engaged with stories as an instructional beginning, and the conceptual focus of lessons expanded to include the interrelationships between Western science concepts and the science that is deeply embedded within stories. Specifically, teachers contemplated the ways in which stories about rock formations provide the foundation of understanding cycles and can scaffold scientific understandings (e.g., carbon, nitrogen, etc.). Joe provided explanations about science concepts from geology, and Tyler drew on his experiences with tribes in the Pacific Northwest to share information about the sociopolitical nature of land rights and their connection to traditional stories. Max often took a pedagogical stance and articulated a claim about stories as a vehicle for outlining scientific inquiries.

As teachers implemented programming, the stances about stories and storytelling that were adopted in the design meeting continued to emerge. Teachers continued to frame storytelling as a way to launch science activities. In addition, teachers reflected on the complex relationship between Western science and Indigenous stories, recognizing that stories are embedded within a network of knowledge practices with specific protocols.

Design Event Two: "Sharing a Story as a Beginning Activity"

Design Context. Four months later, teachers met again to contemplate storytelling as a lesson launch. Between these meetings, teachers continued to implement lessons. All members of the team were present for this meeting, where we continued to build out the larger unit of seeing and representing place. We began by discussing representations, and teachers expressed their concerns about facilitating a conversation with youth that addressed both the content of representations as well as representations as a way of communicating.

Teacher Discourse About Stories. As we planned an introductory lesson on representations, we continued to reflect on the difference between visual representations and stories, in particular the difference between the murals of the Three Sisters story that are displayed in the community center and the story itself (see the figures below).

As the conversation progressed, we also considered other representational forms, including songs and maps. The conversation focused on how to create appropriate scaffolds for youth, so they can both create

The Three Sisters mural is displayed in the main gathering space of the community center. Artwork by Robert Wapahi. Photograph by Warren Perlstein Photography LLC, courtesy of the American Indian Center of Chicago.

Positive Paths, the community center's youth program, designed this mural. It was created using spray paint and is displayed on the second floor of the center, just outside the main room where youth regularly gather. Photograph by Warren Perlstein Photography LLC, courtesy of the American Indian Center of Chicago.

their own representations and read the worldviews embedded within representations:

> ANANDA MARIN: What if you don't even start with the topographic map, maybe that comes later. We can talk about representations and then we can go to the place and say okay, what is in this landscape that's going to help you remember this place? Like if you had to make a map for yourself, what markers would you choose? What plant or tree or whatever do you want to develop a relationship with so that you can come back and read the land?
>
> MEGAN BANG: And maybe it's not even a map. So my point is removing the map very quickly. So the thing that's interesting about this right, is that there's no, the reason I keep thinking about the Three Sisters garden and the Three Sisters mural is because the three sisters story is a representation of a biological phenomenon. It's not a map in a standard kind of map but it is a cultural way of mapping the relationship between three plant species.

In retrospect, both of us were suggesting that our talk about mapping practices was locating maps in Western knowledge systems rather than Indigenous knowledge systems. We implicitly suggested that stories *are* our maps—or more explicitly, models of phenomena; explanations of how things work. Our conversational turns laid the groundwork for us to further reflect on the relationship between stories, maps, and embodied experiences in particular places, or what Cajete (2000) refers to as body sense:

TYLER: For the kids to understand how people make maps . . . Maybe something the kids know, what maps are, they're pretty familiar with the plan. You introduce them to a street map, but then here's the mural. Again it goes to that broader idea of a map. And let them know that even when they look at murals, when they look at, let them know that it's all some type of representation.

ANANDA MARIN: I think that's why we started with, you reminded me of why we came to the rap about the train ride in Chicago, because kids could probably map riding the train. If you ask them to come up with a story about riding the train. They could do that and come up with some sort of map while writing that story right.

Similar to Design Event One, when Tyler made a connection among the elders' everyday stories about places, science processes, and cultural knowledge, here we began to articulate a relationship between youths' everyday experiences across space and time as an opportunity to generate stories in map form. As we continue to develop a lesson on representations, we return to reflect on protocols for knowledge building and stories as a launching activity or instructional beginning:

ANANDA MARIN: No, I guess what I'm saying, so one of Joe's concerns, right, is that the zone maps and the topographic maps present things in sort of like, this dissecting way. So all I guess I'm saying is that, when we go to Bunker Hill with the parents, maybe we should find a story about that place in addition to using zone maps in the scavenger hunt, right, so that they're presented with multiple representations even if we're not talking about representations at that point.

JOE: I agree, I think that would be good. Sharing a story as a beginning activity.

In these two turns, we again see teachers working their way through the pedagogical tensions that emerge when intentionally designing hybrid spaces that bring together Western ways of representing knowledge (topographic maps) and Indigenous ways of representing knowledge (stories).

Summary. Throughout this design event, teachers collectively made sense of stories as representations of and explanations for science phenomena. With this framing in mind, teachers collectively developed pedagogies to engage youth with the community-based practice of storytelling. In addition, teachers continually returned to storytelling as a launching activity and epistemologically framed stories in relation to Western science and Native science. According to Cajete (2000), "stories are alternative ways of understanding relationships, creation, and the creative process itself, as that process is involved in the underlying thought, as well as in how the tales are represented" (p. 44). During this meeting, teachers began to generate a story-driven critique of representations. In other words, teachers articulated a viewpoint of representations as stories, which depict interrelationships between nature and culture across space, time, and place.

As Archibald (2008) describes, land—"earth and its relation, water" (p. 74)—figures centrally in stories and storytelling. A week or so after Design Event Two, we held another design meeting in which we explicitly took up representations of earth layers in traditional stories and rejected elevation as a centering concept. In its place, the importance of land and how habitats support different forms of life became driving concepts. Across these meetings, teachers moved from considering the role of land in understanding elevation, to Western science understandings of elevation, to more relational conceptions of elevation rooted in Indigenous stories. By closely looking at the transcript, we can begin to uncover the ways in which ontology matters in creating hybrid places. We suggest that the teachers are moving toward an articulation of the problem—that starting with simple definitions of scientific concepts such as elevation not only privileges Western understandings but also cedes an ontology of what the different earth layers mean.

Linking Teacher Sense-Making and Community-Based Design Research

Archibald (2008) discusses the many challenges embedded in learning to make meaning from stories, including developing reciprocal relationships with elders, the holders of our traditional stories, and learning to listen to and to tell stories. She poses complex questions about the differences between telling traditional First Nations stories, personal experience stories, and stories that did not originally belong to First Nations peoples but are told in culturally relevant ways. An examination of transcripts from our teacher design meetings indicates that we faced many of the same challenges that Archibald (2008) discusses. Importantly, the issue of how teachers understood story meaning became a productive site of tension.

Our journey with stories was central to our work of reclaiming Indigenous pedagogies and theories. We propose that design meetings served an imaginative function and became a lived-in space where we drew on our everyday and community-based experiences as resources for lesson planning and teaching (Rosebery, 2005; Warren et al., 2001; Zembal-Saul et al., 2000). Participating as decision makers in the design and implementation of curriculum supported our development of new theory and practice from community perspectives. In addition, it opened the space for us, as teachers, to work in relationship with community-based and personal stories (Archibald, 2008). We spontaneously relied on stories as we reflected on issues of knowledge production and representation in the sciences, and this supported our journey in becoming more skilled at navigating between ways of knowing and designing hybrid spaces.

As Brayboy (2005) argues, honoring the "everyday experiences of American Indians" (p. 431) is essential to decolonizing processes. Our efforts toward "storywork," or in this case applying lessons from stories to the development of curricula, became part of a decolonizing pathway. In other words, making meaning with stories allowed us to collectively remember and understand "a worldview embedded in Aboriginal oral traditions" (Archibald, 2008, p. 13). We are not proposing that we reached the ability to make story meaning in a traditional way. However, as teachers, we reclaimed stories as a central part of science and repositioned science teaching and learning from being centered on so-called facts to being centered on processes, practices, and narratives that are co-constructed. In this context, the position of stories in pedagogy was not simply relegated to a realm of culturally appropriate entrance points; instead, we adopted stories as epistemological frames of relational knowledge and knowledge construction.

For us, stories took on the role of Trickster, inviting us to work through the relationship between Western forms of science and Indigenous ways of knowing. We often entered contradictory spaces, where we found our way through the deep and often contrastive intersections between cultural protocols, knowledge generation, relationships (intertribal, intergenerational, nonhuman-centric, etc.), science content, literacy, and orality. Starting from a story in science reconfigures what is privileged in teaching moments from concepts to events happening in time and place. The relationship between stories and pedagogy is not uncomplicated; we often returned to consider the implications that starting with a story might have on the unfolding of subsequent activities.

Discussion and Implications

Teachers of color are not often afforded opportunities to develop pedagogical practices that have the potential of capitalizing on their experiences with and knowledge of students of color—or these opportunities may be educationally and emotionally costly (Brayboy & Maughan, 2009; Montecinos, 2004; Sleeter, 2001). As Brayboy and Maughan (2009) point out, for Indigenous peoples, teacher education has been a "historic site of struggle" (p. 4) where knowledge systems are often in conflict. The overwhelming emphasis placed on Whiteness in teacher education comes at a cost; namely, that teacher candidates of color often feel underrepresented and underprepared (Au & Blake, 2003; Montecinos, 2004; Sleeter, 2001; Villegas & Lucas, 2004). Richardson and Villenas (2000)—drawing on the works of Indigenous scholars such as Vine Deloria Jr., Gerald Vizenor, and Robert Allen Warrior—call us to shift our line of vision toward investing in community-based power and traditions. This may require a shifting conception of our basic notions of what it looks like and means to be a "teacher." Ball (1995) suggests that taking a close look at out-of-school environments allows researchers to move away from narrow conceptions of teaching and learning and creates opportunities in which practitioners and researchers alike can reexamine "diversity and reform in education" (p. 129). An important question arises when focusing on informal learning environments: What happens when we "separate our pedagogy from the traditional pedagogue" (Ball, 1995, p. 144)? We argue that CBDR is one site to explore this question. Further, we suggest that CBDR supports teachers in resurrecting our senses of self and our ways of being on the land, which move us toward relationally centered and ultimately transformational meanings of Indigeneity.

Ananda Marin *(Choctaw, African American, and European American descent) is a postdoctoral fellow in the Psychology Department at Northwestern University.*

Megan Bang *(Ojibwe and Italian descent) is assistant professor in educational psychology at the University of Washington.*

NOTE

This research was supported by a grant from the National Science Foundation (Award Number 0815112). We are grateful to all of the community members, teachers, designers, and research assistants who participated in this work. In particular, we wish to thank the teachers who collaborated with us.

REFERENCES

Aikenhead, G. S. (1997). Toward a First Nations cross-cultural science and technology curriculum. *Science Education, 81*(2), 217–238.

American Association for the Advancement of Science/Project 2061. (1993). *Benchmarks for science literacy.* New York, NY: Oxford University Press.

Archibald, J. (2008). *Indigenous storywork.* Vancouver, Canada: University of British Columbia Press.

Au, K. H., & Blake, K. M. (2003). Cultural identity and learning to teach in a diverse community: Findings from a collective case study. *Journal of Teacher Education, 54*(3), 192–205.

Ball, A. F. (1995). Community-based learning in urban settings as a model for educational reform. *Applied Behavioral Science Review, 3*(2), 127–146.

Bang, M. (2008). *Understanding students' epistemologies: Examining practice and meaning in community contexts* (Unpublished doctoral dissertation). Northwestern University, Evanston, IL.

Bang, M., & Medin, D. (2010). Cultural processes in science education: Supporting the navigation of multiple epistemologies. *Science Education, 94*(6), 1008–1026.

Bang, M., Medin, D., Washinawatok, K., & Chapman, S. (2010). Innovations in culturally-based science education through partnerships and community. In M. Khine & I. Saleh (Eds.), *New science of learning: Cognition, computers and collaboration in education* (pp. 569–592). New York, NY: Springer.

Barnhardt, R., & Kawagley, A. O. (2005). Indigenous knowledge systems and Alaska Native ways of knowing. *Anthropology and Education Quarterly, 36*(1), 8–23.

Battiste, M. (2002). *Indigenous knowledge and pedagogy in First Nations education: A literature review with recommendations.* Eskasoni, Canada: Apamuwek Institute.

Brayboy, B. (2005). Toward a tribal critical race theory in education. *The Urban Review, 37*(5), 425–446.

Brayboy, B. M. J., & Maughan, E. (2009). Indigenous knowledges and the story of the bean. *Harvard Educational Review, 79*(1), 1–21.

Brown, A. L. (1992). Design experiments: Theoretical and methodological challenges in creating complex interventions in classroom settings. *The Journal of the Learning Sciences, 2*(2), 141–178.

Cajete, G. A. (2000). *Native science: Natural laws of interdependence.* Santa Fe, NM: Clear Light.
Cajete, G. A. (2005). American Indian epistemologies. *New Directions for Student Services, 109,* 69–78.
Collins, A., Joseph, D., & Bielaczyc, K. (2004). Design research: Theoretical and methodological issues. *The Journal of the Learning Sciences, 13*(1), 15–42.
Davis, E. A., Petish, D., & Smithey, J. (2006). Challenges new science teachers face. *Review of Educational Research, 76*(4), 607–651.
Deloria, V. (1979). *The metaphysics of modern existence.* San Francisco, CA: Harper & Row.
Deloria, V. (1997). *Red earth, white lies: Native Americans and the myths of scientific fact.* Golden, CO: Fulcrum.
Deloria, V., & Wildcat, D. (2001). *Power and place: Indian education in America.* Golden, CO: Fulcrum.
Design-Based Research Collaborative. (2003). Design-based research: An emerging paradigm for educational inquiry. *Educational Researcher, 32*(1), 5–8.
Duran, B., Duran, E., & Yellow Horse Brave Heart, M. (1998). Native Americans and the trauma of history. In R. Thornton (Ed.), *Studying Native America: Problems and prospects* (pp. 60–76). Madison: University of Wisconsin Press.
Elby, A., & Hammer, D. (2010). Epistemological resources and framing: A cognitive framework for helping teachers interpret and respond to their students' epistemologies. In L. D. Bendixen & F. C. Feucht (Eds.), *Personal epistemology in the classroom: Theory, research, and implications for practice* (pp. 409–434). New York, NY: Cambridge University Press.
Gutierrez, K. D., Baquedano-Lopez, P., & Tejeda, C. (1999). Rethinking diversity: Hybridity and hybrid language practices in the third space. *Mind, Culture, and Activity, 6*(4), 286–303.
Jackson, K., Garrison, A., Wilson, J., Gibbons, L., & Shahan, E. (2013). Exploring relationships between setting up complex tasks and opportunities to learn in concluding whole-class discussions in middle-grades mathematics instruction. *Journal for Research in Mathematics Education, 44*(4), 646–682.
Kawagley, O. (1995). *A Yupiaq worldview.* Prospect Heights, IL: Waveland Press.
Lee, C. D. (2001). Is October Brown Chinese? A cultural modeling activity system for underachieving students. *American Educational Research Journal, 38*(1), 97–141.
Leonard, B. (2008). Mediating Athabascan oral traditions in postsecondary classrooms. *International Journal of Multicultural Education, 10*(2). Retrieved from http://journals.sfu.ca/ijme/index.php/ijme/article/viewFile/126/227
Maaka, M., Au, K. H., Lefcourt, Y. K., & Bogac, L. P. (2001). "Raccoon? Wass dat?" Hawaiian preservice teachers reconceptualize culture, literacy, and schooling. In P. R. Schmidt & P. B. Mosenthal (Eds.), *Reconceptualizing literacy in the new age of multiculturalism and pluralism* (pp. 341–366). Greenwich, CT: Information Age.
McCarty, T. L., & Lee, T. S. (2014). Critical culturally sustaining/revitalizing pedagogy and Indigenous education sovereignty. *Harvard Educational Review, 84*(1), 101–124.

Moll, L. C., Amanti, C., Neff, D., & Gonzalez, N. (1992). Funds of knowledge for teaching: Using a qualitative approach to connect homes and schools. *Theory Into Practice, 31*(2), 132–141.

Montecinos, C. (2004). Paradoxes in multicultural teacher education research: Students of color positioned as objects while ignored as subjects. *International Journal of Qualitative Studies in Education, 17*(2), 167–181.

Nasir, N. S., Rosebery, A. S., Warren, B., & Lee, C. D. (2006). Learning as a cultural process: Achieving equity through diversity. In R. Keith Sawyer (Ed.), *The Cambridge handbook of the learning sciences* (pp. 489–504). New York, NY: Cambridge University Press.

National Research Council. (2009). *Learning science in informal environments: People, places, and pursuits.* (Committee on Learning Science in Informal Environments. Board on Science Education, Division of Behavioral and Social Sciences and Education). Washington, DC: The National Academies Press.

National Research Council. (2012). *A framework for K–12 science education: Practices, crosscutting concepts, and core ideas.* (Committee on a Conceptual Framework for New K-12 Science Education Standards. Board on Science Education, Division of Behavioral and Social Sciences and Education). Washington, DC: The National Academies Press.

Nelson-Barber, S., & Estrin, E. T. (1995). Bringing Native American perspectives to mathematics and science teaching. *Theory Into Practice, 34*(3), 174–185.

Ochs, E., Taylor, C., Rudolph, D., & Smith, R. (1992). Storytelling as a theory-building activity. *Discourse Processes, 15*(1), 37–72.

Richardson, T. (2011). Navigating the problem of inclusion as enclosure in Native culture-based education: Theorizing shadow curriculum. *Curriculum Inquiry, 41*(3), 332–349.

Richardson, T., & Villenas, S. (2000). "Other" encounters: Dances with whiteness in multicultural education. *Educational Theory, 50*(2), 255–273.

Rosebery, A. S. (2005). "What are we going to do next?": Lesson planning as a resource for teaching. In R. Nemirovsky, A. S. Rosebery, J. Solomon, & B. Warren (Eds.), *Everyday matters in science and mathematics: Studies of complex classroom events* (pp. 299–327). Mahwah, NJ: Erlbaum.

Rosebery, A. S., Warren, B., & Conant, F. (1992). Appropriating scientific discourse: Findings from language minority classrooms. *Journal of the Learning Sciences, 2*, 61–94.

Sleeter, C. E. (2001). Preparing teachers for culturally diverse schools: Research and the overwhelming presence of whiteness. *Journal of Teacher Education, 52*(2), 94–106.

Smith, L. T. (1999). *Decolonizing methodologies: Research and indigenous peoples.* New York, NY: Zed Books.

Smith, L. T., Smith, G. H., Boler, M., Kempton, M., Ormond, A., Chueh, H. C., & Waetford, R. (2002). "Do you guys hate Aucklanders too?" Youth: Voicing difference from the rural heartland. *Journal of Rural Studies, 18*(2), 169–178.

Stein, M. K., Engle, R. A., Smith, M. S., & Hughes, E. K. (2008). Orchestrating productive mathematical discussions: Five practices for helping teachers move beyond show and tell. *Mathematical Thinking and Learning, 10*(4), 313–340.

Stein, M. K., Grover, B. W., & Henningsen, M. (1996). Building student capacity for mathematical thinking and reasoning: An analysis of mathematical tasks used in reform classrooms. *American Educational Research Journal, 33*(2), 455–488.

Tippeconnic III, J. (1999). Tribal control of American Indian education: Observations since the 1960s with implications for the future. In K. Swisher & J. Tippeconnic (Eds.), *Next steps: Research and practice to advance Indian education* (pp. 3–52). Washington, DC: Office of Educational Research and Improvement (ERIC Document #ED 427 902).

Tuck, E. (2009). Suspending damage: A letter to communities. *Harvard Educational Review, 79*(3), 409–427.

Van de Walle, J. A., Folk, S., Karp, K. S., & Bay-Williams, J. M. (2010). *Elementary and middle school mathematics: Teaching developmentally.* Upper Saddle River, NJ: Pearson Education.

Villegas, A., & Lucas, T. (2004). Diversifying the teacher workforce: A retrospective and prospective analysis. *Yearbook of the National Society for the Study of Education, 103*(1), 70–104.

Warren, B., Ballenger, C., Ogonowski, M., Rosebery, A. S., & Hudicourt-Barnes, J. (2001). Rethinking diversity in learning science: The logic of everyday sense-making. *Journal of Research in Science Teaching, 38*(5), 529–552.

Yazzie-Mintz, T. (2007). From a place deep inside: Culturally appropriate curriculum as the embodiment of Navajo-ness in classroom pedagogy. *Journal of American Indian Education, 46*(3), 72–93.

Zembal-Saul, C., Blumenfeld, P., & Krajcik, J. (2000). Influence of guided cycles of planning, teaching, and reflection on prospective elementary teachers' science content representations. *Journal of Research in Science Teaching, 37*(4), 318–339.

Reports From the Field

Aboriginal Perspectives and Issues in Teacher Education

MATTHEW ETHERINGTON

This article reports on an Aboriginal Issues in Education course for fourth-year preservice teachers at a Canadian university in British Columbia, including the rationale behind the course, the course content, the main issues raised, and the final course performance examination before a panel of Aboriginal elders. The course experience suggests that cognitive and moral transformation in students can occur if the classroom is a place of cognitive and moral tension, and a pedagogical approach to learning develops and promotes cultural bridges of understanding between Aboriginal and European ways of learning. The article concludes with recommendations for instructors of Aboriginal courses.

IN ORDER TO COMPETENTLY ENGAGE with cultural diversity in Canada, K–12 preservice teachers need to confront personal prejudices and deal with misconceptions about Aboriginal peoples and education. Teacher training must guide them through these processes. Research by Finney and Orr (1995) concludes that "serious prejudices and misunderstandings exist within the attitudes and beliefs of non-Aboriginal teacher education students in relation to persons of Aboriginal ancestry" (p. 327).

An education course *on* Aboriginal peoples must be an experience *with* Aboriginal people. To transform understanding and practice, non-Aboriginal preservice teachers must experience a personal conflict of heart and mind. Tanaka (2009) notes that for change to occur, non-Aboriginal preservice teachers must experience "vulnerability and attention to emotions and passions" (p. 213). Since most teachers are monocultural, Tanaka (2009) suggests disturbing Eurocentric perspectives (see also McInerney & Van Etten, 2002). The course described here, EDUC 496, Issues in Indigenous Education, aims to disturb and challenge non-Aboriginal preservice teachers' stereotypical ways of thinking about Aboriginal people in order to lead to a change of heart and mind. The general consensus in scholarship is that Canadian institutions of learning have not taken seriously the Aboriginal perspectives on pedagogy and worldview that require students to experience personal conflict leading to transformation. Rasmussen, Baydala, and Shennan (2004) suggest that school systems still use instructional methods consistent with dominant cultural patterns. Similarly, Tanaka (2009) describes Aboriginal preservice teacher education programs as insulated interventions.

This article describes an undergraduate education course in Aboriginal issues designed for fourth-year preservice teachers and how it benefitted from the presence of Aboriginal people and an emphasis on conflict and personal transformation using a performance examination.[1] Transformation included the teachers cultivating situations in which learning is purposefully interrupted by demanding cognitive and moral experiences that change their outlook on the world (English, 2011). We should want nothing less than total transformation *with* the oppressed (Freire, 2005). Transformation of the oppressed is elicited by those in positions of power, such as schoolteachers. Teachers must confront prejudices and typecasts of Aboriginal people in order to develop a just education system. Justice requires that Aboriginal people exercise their inherent rights and flourish fully as human beings.

The Rationale Behind an Aboriginal Course in Education

In 2011, the opportunity arose to develop an Aboriginal issues in education course in conversation with Aboriginal partners and participants. In 2012, the School of Education included the first Aboriginal education course as a core requirement for graduating K–12 classroom teachers. The 6-week course served 51 fourth-year preservice teachers and was grounded in Aboriginal pedagogy.

As a non-Aboriginal person, I recognize that my knowledge and experience is limited. However, Craven (2003) suggests that a fundamental requirement for instructors of Aboriginal studies courses is to consult with local Aboriginal communities to develop curriculum. This course was designed in close partnership with Aboriginal educators from the First Nations Education Steering Committee (FNESC), with Aboriginal educators from the British Columbia Teachers' Federation, and with the university *Siya:m.*[2] In addition, an Aboriginal person was invited to teach in almost every class meeting to emphasize a First Nations voice and perspective.

Consultation on course curriculum, resources, and pedagogy was carried out with the approval of Aboriginal leaders and educators. As the program grows and faculty are expanded, the School of Education is committed to hiring Aboriginal colleagues and instructors. As a non-Aboriginal instructor, I was encouraged by Viri (2003), who advised that although we desperately need Native teachers as facilitators and agents of change in our communities, "we must also acknowledge that a good, sensitive and effective teacher can be a member of any race" (p. 37).

In 2010, the FNESC, an independent society committed to improving education for all First Nations learners in British Columbia (BC), commended the BC College of Teachers for passing new regulations requiring all applicants for certification as a teacher in British Columbia to receive specialized training in Aboriginal education (First Nations Education Steering Committee, 2010). In a letter to the BC Ministry of Education regarding its Proposed Directions for Graduation, the FNESC encouraged the ministry to require that a course in Aboriginal studies be a part of graduation requirements for all students in British Columbia. As of 2014, all BC universities offer teacher education degrees that include mandatory two-credit and three-credit Aboriginal education courses. McInerney and Van Etten (2002) maintain that all people have the right to learn the true history of their country, so mandatory Aboriginal education in Canada is a critical component of every teacher's education.

The aim of EDUC 496, Issues in Indigenous Education, is to bring the preservice teachers to a point of personal conflict concerning their own views and beliefs regarding Aboriginal education and then to cognitive and moral transformation. The course took a different position than Craven (2003), who suggests that a successful mandatory Aboriginal course for preservice teachers should have all positive and no negative student evaluations. I wanted the preservice teachers to value the course; to receive it with an open heart and mind and a commitment to include Aboriginal perspectives throughout the entire school curriculum. However, my consultations with Aboriginal leaders prior to the course suggested that in order to achieve this goal, some suffering would be required, which would not necessarily lead to positive student evaluations. Similarly, Lingenfelter and Lingenfelter (2003) maintain that moral growth requires suffering; that in order to understand another culture, teachers must surrender some of their own cultural prejudice. In other words, they must develop two sets of eyes to see with (Tanaka, 2009).

The course was designed to promote Aboriginal perspectives, with an inside perspective on Aboriginal pedagogy. Nord (2010) describes the inside perspective:

> If we are to understand different cultures, we must be able to get inside them. How do they understand things like pedagogy, not, how do we understand them given our preconceptions and values? If we screen alternative traditions through our own conceptual filter (assuming that we know how to interpret the world) we will gain no critical perspective on our own assumptions. (p. 110)

EDUC 496 incorporated Elder teachings, Aboriginal content and perspectives, and the use of Native language in the classroom. There were nine Aboriginal speakers invited as guests to the classroom, averaging one to two speakers every week. As a non-Aboriginal instructor, I found it critical to include the voices of Aboriginal people. Topics on violence and oppression are often abstract to those not affected until the faces and the voices of the victims are before us (Wolterstorff, 2008). At the beginning of each class, protocol was modeled by the instructor in acknowledging the host community, its people, and its territory. Protocol was used by the preservice teachers at the beginning of their performance examination. When an Aboriginal speaker or Aboriginal elder attended the class, they were welcomed as teachers, and the preservice teachers and the instructor were acknowledged as learners. At the conclusion of each class, the Aboriginal speakers and elders were presented with a gift of appreciation by one of the preservice teachers. On one occasion, the elders received tobacco.[3] The Aboriginal speakers and the Aboriginal elders were invited by contacting the Aboriginal educators at the BC Teachers' Federation.

The course syllabus was formed from the recommendation of a number of Aboriginal voices. These included Aboriginal educators from the FNESC in Vancouver, British Columbia, and also the university Siya:m. The syllabus was presented as a fluid document that continues to be informed by Aboriginal voices and experiences. In this course, Aboriginal people were invited to speak and teach the class, for as John Stuart Mill asserts in *On Liberty*:

> We must hear arguments from persons who actually believe and live them. For 99 out of 100 persons have never thrown themselves into the

position of those who think differently from them, and as a consequence they do not know the doctrine which they themselves profane. (1974/1859, p. 98)

If teacher educators really want to change a deficit view of Aboriginal peoples, Tanaka (2009) suggests that they need to walk deeply alongside. She notes that even service projects in which preservice teachers interact with Aboriginal people simply to give them things creates a false and misguided view of having made a difference.

Therefore, the course was designed to offer Aboriginal knowledge of Aboriginal issues and pedagogy. Additionally, the course aimed to examine and confront student teachers' preconceptions regarding Aboriginal people and education.

Course Design

One way to honor Aboriginal realities is to highlight the difference between acts of benevolence (doing good) and justice (inherent rights). The voices and lived experiences of Aboriginal people affected by Canada's colonial past spoke powerfully to that contrast. One or two Aboriginal speakers were invited each week for the 6-week duration of the course. Dion (2009) writes that building relationships between non-Aboriginal and Aboriginal people means making non-Aboriginal people cognizant of Aboriginal stories. Inviting Aboriginal people to the classroom kindled a serious Aboriginal perspective of story sharing. Nine Aboriginal leaders shared their stories and experiences with the preservice teachers. Importantly, they sought to establish positive relationships with the education students because there were no Aboriginal faculty available to teach this course. However, the course did benefit greatly from the university Siya:m. The Siya:m frequently attended classes, shared her history and experience, offered guidance, and developed trust with the preservice teachers.

The course addressed six themes, confirmed as applicable to a BC Canadian context by the FNESC: (1) A Selective Overview of Research on Critical Issues in Aboriginal Pedagogy: Myths, Facts, and Issues; (2) Narrative as Pedagogy; (3) Ceremony as Pedagogy; (4) Children as Learners; (5) An Overview of Teaching Methods; and (6) The Elders as Source and Authority in Pedagogy. The themes required a very personal commitment by the preservice teachers to keep an open heart and mind and allow themselves to learn and understand from the perspectives and lived stories of the Aboriginal instructors. The preservice teachers were also asked to participate fully as learners in the food ceremonies, name-giving ceremonies, totem pole constructions, shared puppet activities, oral storytelling, culture sharing, cedar wood carving, and weekly sharing circles. The weekly activities were grounded in the notion of shared participation with others while also experiencing ways of knowing that were initially foreign.

Critical Issues Raised in Class: Knowledge, Equality and Justice, Forgiveness, Benevolence

The following controversial topics elicited discussion and conflict throughout the course.

Knowledge

One of the most controversial issues raised by the preservice teachers was the discussion about Aboriginal knowledge and Western knowledge. Many of the preservice teachers had learned a Eurocentric version of Aboriginal people, focusing on clothing, foods, and ceremonies. However, this knowledge contrasted with the lived experience of being an Aboriginal person in Canada. The contrast was raised when the preservice teachers recognized that some types of knowledge are silenced and some types are privileged, to the detriment of others. One preservice teacher commented, "We never addressed the residential school story at school or that darker side of history. I only remember learning about some of the ceremonies that First Nation people participate [in]."

It was evident through class discussions that Aboriginal knowledge shared as a lived experience of suffering, injustices, or even perspectives was silenced at school. School had offered caricatures or romanticized versions of Aboriginal people and lifestyles. One preservice teacher acknowledged, "It would have been easy to believe that all Aboriginal people dressed the same way and lived in tee-pees." However, other preservice teachers expressed an attitude of having "heard this all before." One preservice teacher remarked, "We did this in high school, so I know it [residential schools] already." When asked what they had "heard before," one preservice teacher commented, "Before we judge all the teachers in these schools, many teachers were trying to help Aboriginal children for the future."

Inviting Aboriginal speakers to the class provided an opportunity for the preservice teachers to wrestle through the normalization of privileged ideas, values, and beliefs embedded through a Eurocentric K–12 school experience. This was evident when two Elders shared their lived residential school experience in class. Recording the word "abuse" on the whiteboard and asking the preservice teachers to give comparative words representing cruelty and mistreatment, the Elders compelled the teachers to recognize a reality of history that school had hidden from them.

For the next week, I received an assortment of e-mails from the preservice teachers regarding this experience. One wrote, "I am finding this class really difficult, I am just hanging in there." Another shared in relation to residential schools, "I can now see the difference between Aboriginal knowledge and western knowledge." She continued, "I grew up in Alberta [Canada] where Aboriginal people are represented as drunks with no jobs or incentive. My family even share these views. The Elders told a different story. I recently shared this different story told by the Elders with my parents." And finally, the Elders' lived residential school experience was too overwhelming for one preservice teacher. At the end of the class, he stayed back to speak with the Elders. Sobbing but trying to hold back the tears, he apologized for the abuses against Aboriginal people and then fell at the Elders' feet, pleading for forgiveness. However, this was not the experience of all. In the postreflection, one preservice teacher wrote, "I was made to feel guilty in this class so I was just pretending [to agree]." I shared this comment with one of the Aboriginal speakers, who addressed it during the next class. "Such collective guilt," the speaker said, "has created in some a sense of helplessness; however guilt has no place in reconciliation."

The university Siya:m shared a story about a grade 3 Aboriginal student who requested that the Siya:m speak to the student's class about residential schools. The teacher denied her the opportunity. Most of the preservice teachers agreed that the class teacher was within her rights to deny permission. One preservice teacher commented, "The residential school story is not an appropriate topic for grade three children." In response, the university Siya:m noted that "denying the child their right to teach Canadian history demonstrates that an Aboriginal perspective of Canadian history is unwelcome." Aboriginal knowledge is, as one Aboriginal speaker said, "knowledge that non-Aboriginal people are excluded from having." One preservice teacher justified the silencing of Aboriginal knowledge: "There is some knowledge concerning Canadian history that should be postponed from school students until the 'appropriate' time."

Learning the true Aboriginal history of Canada from Aboriginal people is perceived as "dangerous" knowledge. Some preservice teachers maintained that, although important, knowledge of Canada's colonial past, shared through the lived experience of Aboriginal people, should at least be carefully filtered. One preservice teacher remarked, "We do have lots of Aboriginal content already in the curriculum and I will teach it through the curriculum as any teacher would." Lomawaima and McCarty (2006) argue that certain Indigenous educational policies and practices are deemed safe because they pose no threat to U.S. identity or economic superiority while at other times similar policies and practices are considered a threat and therefore perceived as dangerous.

Equality and Justice

With regard to equality, Battiste (2013) argues that "students have absorbed one aspect of the term equality, thinking that everyone was and is equal to receiving services and education in Canada" (p. 126). Aboriginal scholars largely agree that the equality discourse has shut down justice talk and is another form of oppression experienced by Aboriginal people (St. Denis, 2013). The Nobel Prize–winning economist Amatrya Sen points out that "everyone is for equality; it's just that what constitutes equality for one is not the same as for the other" (as cited in Ladson-Billings, 2004, p.27).

The preservice teachers were wedded to a Eurocentric notion of *equality*, often commenting that "everyone should be treated equally." Many agreed that this notion of equality is applied when working with Aboriginal and non-Aboriginal school students. As one preservice teacher wrote on the course evaluation, "As a teacher I will not have any favorites." Finney and Orr (1995) argue that despite the goodwill of teacher education students holding this view, it reveals an individualistic approach to social change that presupposes that broader and systematic societal barriers do not exist for Aboriginal people. As another preservice teacher remarked, "Aboriginal people are just like everyone else." With an oversimplified notion of equality, "teacher educators may be creating a generation of teachers who move from unrealistic optimism to cynicism and despair" (Finney & Orr, 1995, p. 331).

Justice recognizes past wrongs; the importance of agency and autonomy; and "takes into account larger, social, economic and political variables affecting schools" (Kanu, 2006, p. 1). Justice and not equality welcomes difference (see Egea-Kuehne, 2008). Justice in education advances the inclusion of Aboriginal perspectives at an epistemological level (Denzin, Lincoln, & Smith, 2008). Justice requires rendering "non-Aboriginal people cognizant of our stories and engaging teachers and students with speaking to three hundred years of oppression" (Dion, 2009, p. 76).

In class, the Aboriginal speakers spoke of justice as respect for the inherent and sovereign rights and worth of Aboriginal people, including their knowledge, values, understandings, and worldview (see also St. Denis, 2013). Although the preservice teachers preferred to speak of equality, the Aboriginal speakers spoke of justice as a relationship, an open hand of hospitality, and a responsibility to one's neighbor (see also Martin, 2008). The importance of forming deep relationships and "a braided act of walking-alongside Aboriginal people" (see Tanaka, 2009, p. 225) did become important to the preservice teachers over time. One teacher wrote, "This course saved me. As a teacher I need to involve Aboriginal people in the planning." Another teacher revealed that she had, for the first time, sought guidance from an Aboriginal person (the university Siya:m) to develop a culturally sensitive lesson for a class project.

However, two preservice teachers refused to move away from the equality discourse in multicultural Canada, where giving any one group additional privileges is deemed unjust. One argued in class, "What about the Japanese or the Chinese? What gives Aboriginal people additional privileges—being here first?—I don't see that being a good enough reason." Another preservice teacher wrote, "I don't know why we needed a whole course in Aboriginal education, it doesn't seem fair to others?" Finney and Orr (1995) suggest that the "equal discourse" is harmful to the welfare of marginalized groups while Battiste (2013) argues that "Canadians have accepted a self-narrative description of themselves as generous, having overcome earlier bigotries and prejudices" (p. 125).

However, Viri (2003) notes that if change and improvement are to occur, Native issues should be embedded within a multicultural framework. Many of the preservice teachers were comfortable with a focus on multiculturalism but not Aboriginal sovereignty. However, the Aboriginal leaders I consulted disagreed, arguing that multiculturalism and Aboriginal issues are different.

The multicultural discourses, St. Denis (2013) argues, are devoted to the notion of equality and "have been evoked to manage and silence conversations about First Nation perspectives in the school curriculum" (p. 28). While in a number of countries "teacher education curricula seem to embrace equality under the guise of Multicultural

Studies (e.g., Australia, USA), Aboriginal Studies have not been afforded the same status" (Craven, 2003, p. 166). Ladson-Billings (2004) uses the idea of "big tent multiculturalism" to highlight how ineffective multiculturalism is for Aboriginal people because it ignores justice talk.

The preservice teachers fused multicultural issues with Aboriginal issues by highlighting the importance of "equality, tolerance, and fairness." This was significant because it allowed them to ignore justice as a rubric to determine if a sovereign people with treaty rights are given space in education policy and a crowded Eurocentric curriculum. Reconciliation efforts in education must therefore focus on justice—not just equality, apologies, guilt, and pardons. Justice in Aboriginal education is the only way forward (Smith, 2011).

Apology and Forgiveness

Jurisdictions across Australia, the United States, South Africa, and Canada have made efforts to lead what Miyagawa (2012) calls "the sorry parade." Examples of government apologies to Aboriginal people leading to forgiveness of the oppressor and eventual reconciliation were a persistent topic of debate in the course. One preservice teacher stated, "What about forgiveness? We *are* sorry and we said it publically. Forgiveness should mean that we now look to the future, not backwards." Another preservice teacher asked, "The prime minister apologized so why do we have to prioritize First Nations people? What about other groups in Canada?" These comments revealed increasing tension within the hearts and the minds of the preservice teachers.

I was interested in the words they used: *prioritize, forgive,* and *future.* What did these words really mean to them? It had already been suggested that apologies and forgiveness can often lead to taking no further responsibility for nurturing Aboriginal autonomy. For the great educator of justice Emmanuel Levinas, forgiveness meant no justice and a lack of responsibility (see Egea-Kuehne, 2008). One preservice teacher acknowledged that apologies mean "we are free of guilt, but Aboriginal people are still wronged." What is the oppressor's moral condition now? Has the victim been relieved of having been wronged? The class agreed that apologies do not change the fact that Aboriginal people are still in the same position as before the apology. Similarly, Wolterstorff (2008) suggests that apologies and forgiveness "deal with guilt, not with being wronged" (p. 9). The oppressor dimension is attended to, but what about the abused? It seems apology acts are designed to "allow public officials to apologize without incurring legal liability" (Miyagawa, 2012, p. 182). Many of the preservice teachers understood a notion of apology and forgiveness that did not entail a process that embraced cooperation or collaboration with Aboriginal people. This was confirmed by one preservice teacher who expressed his frustration: "If they would just tell us exactly what they want. South Africa's Indigenous peoples have done this already. But we always seem to do the wrong thing and then get criticized." If forgiveness and apology are to be lived out, preservice teachers need a broader understanding that involves a holistic process for thinking, communicating, and acting—not in isolation but together.

Benevolence

The fourth issue raised in class was benevolence. The preservice teachers were committed to the colonial mindset of benevolence. Benevolence is the desire to assist, be generous, or do good to another (Collins & Nolan, 2005). The current preoccupation of the government of Canada is with "doing something" about First Nations issues (Crowley & Coates, 2012). Benevolence assumes minorities can be improved or helped to become like the majority (Stove, 2011). The preservice teachers were challenged to consider this problem: that benevolence ignores differences because it focuses on uniformity.

The preservice teachers often talked in terms of benevolence and did so in terms of good behavior and bad behavior, better and worse. One preservice teacher responded: "We are already committed as teachers to help all our students including Aboriginal people." One Aboriginal speaker reminded the class about an incident in 2006, when a teaching assistant in Thunder Bay, Ontario, tried to "help" a 7-year-old Aboriginal student in the name of benevolence by cutting off his hair so he could look like everyone else. The preservice teachers agreed that this was a return to the trauma of residential school. One preservice teacher confessed that the school experience shared by the Aboriginal speakers in class had altered his perception of "doing good" as a future teacher. "Being a great teacher," he said, "is about listening to Aboriginal people."

In response to the perceived view of Canadians as a good and benevolent people, one preservice teacher wrote a poem to the Elders that included the following words: "We destroyed your culture, and we destroyed your soul, now we can only ask your forgiveness and allow you to show us how." Another preservice teacher made a parallel between the persecution of Irish Catholics and Aboriginal peoples in the name of "benevolence." He reflected that "the menace of the Irish race to the Scottish Nationality saw persecution and assimilation to the protestant Scottish race by one dominant group trying to 'help' another culture with the goal of devastating those people." The Aboriginal speakers also shared their new insights gained as a result of the preservice teachers' observations. At the conclusion of the course, one Aboriginal speaker wrote, "Some get it and some don't," while another agreed, "It is obvious that the students are at very different levels of moral growth."

The Performance-Based Learning Examination

The preservice teachers were required to participate in a performance-based examination to be held at the conclusion of the course on a Saturday from 9:00 a.m. to 4:00 p.m. The examination required the preservice teachers to show their personal conflict, evidence of transformation, and moral growth to a panel of Aboriginal elders. Apart from the course instructor, the judges were Aboriginal people who had visited and shared with the class during the semester. The performance exam was also an opportunity for the preservice teachers to give something back to the speakers as a token of gratitude. The preservice teachers were asked to perform by themselves in a creative way—and probably out of their comfort zone. Themes presented included ideas related to reconciliation, truth, justice, human flourishing, and responsibility.

The performance examination required the preservice teachers to wrestle with and reexamine the ideas and knowledge discussed throughout the 6 weeks of the course. Moreover, they had to confront their own learning journey and demonstrate their new knowledge and transformation in a culturally sensitive way. Lingenfelter and Lingenfelter (2003) note that the goal of this type of exam is to learn in a more meaningful and holistic way; to present ideas face-to-face rather than simply write about them, which is the dominant Eurocentric model of learning.

The performance final offered the judges and the judged the opportunity to observe the preservice teachers' reactions to dissonance and to consider the character attributes that might determine cross-cultural understanding and practice.

Many of the preservice teachers performed in a manner that was uncomfortable or foreign to them. For example, one preservice teacher, a self-professed nondancer, completed the performance examination as a dance to demonstrate his willingness to learn and grow. A nonpainter chose to paint a harrowing depiction of the residential school experience

A holistic medicine wheel, created for the performance examination by student Ursula Neuscheler, who describes it: "The wheel portrays a tree, symbol of the First Nations of Canada. The roots show how ancient their culture is, the full foliage shows that First Nations people are healthy and vibrant."

in real time. Another preservice teacher washed the feet of the Elders as an act of humility and performed a song about hope and reconciliation. The preservice teachers were assessed by the judges using a 5-point rubric, as shown in the figure below.

The performance examination was demanding for the preservice teachers because it was difficult to discern how to show conflict and a transformation of heart and mind. As challenging as it was, the performance exam provided an authentic and honest platform for transparency. The tears that flowed freely from the eyes of the preservice teachers were a sign of unity, hope, and understanding. One preservice teacher shared how the Aboriginal speakers had reminded her of the importance of family. For most of the presentation she wept. One of the judges asked about the origin of her tears. The residential school had been a reminder to her of the importance of her aging grandfather and the impact his eventual loss would incur on the family. The performance exam allowed

Panelist name: Student name:	Poor	Fair	Good	Excellent
1. Aboriginal knowledge and perspectives are evident				
2. Awareness of personal conflict and evidence of transformation/growth				
3. Culturally inclusive pedagogy (i.e., story, poetry, dance, song)				
4. Spiritual themes are evident (e.g., image reflector, community server, Creator worshiper, creation caretakers, order discoverers, temple keepers, beauty creators, idolatry discerners, truth seekers)				
5. Enthusiastic/passionate				
Total: **Comments:**				

Performance examination rubric

this future teacher to experience and display a sense of solidarity *with* the losses that Aboriginal people have experienced.

One preservice teacher wrote and performed a rap song about her transformation in the course, a performance that impressed the judges. One judge wrote on her scoring rubric, "This was a transformation of ideas and perceptions of Aboriginal people." Another panel judge wrote, "This student's emotion was sincere, very moving, powerful" while another panel judge recorded, "Artistry integrated in delivery of political consciousness raising." A further comment included, "This was a presentation of developing empathy for others versus the self." And finally, "This student [performance] shows the redemptive power of storytelling, reciprocal, rather than just being a consumer." One panel judge remarked, "The performance exam helped me appreciate the emotional obstacles that teachers experience in relation to reconciliation." Another judge commented, "It is face-to-face experiences like these that will help transform the hearts and minds of future teachers."

After the performance exam, one of the judges e-mailed the following sentiments: "I found the presentations, several in particular, very powerful and I would recommend this format again. I think this structure creates an emotional response, something that I don't think they will ever forget. I remember the comments from students on how this class really shifted their perspectives and would change how they approached teaching."

Concluding Thoughts

This mandatory Aboriginal course in a teacher education program aimed to challenge and interrupt the norms of conventional practice in order to help preservice teachers become more sensitive and insightful regarding Aboriginal issues, values, and worldviews. The course was grounded in Aboriginal pedagogy and perspectives and structured to include a live performance examination in the presence of Aboriginal leaders. Although the course was facilitated by a non-Aboriginal person, an Aboriginal person taught nearly every class. Non-Aboriginal educators must seek positive relationships with Aboriginal people and draw on their wisdom, traditions, and knowledge. As Tanaka (2009) maintains, this involves walking alongside Aboriginal people in feeling, thought, and action.

The experience of teaching one mandatory Aboriginal course to non-Aboriginal preservice teachers suggests that the classroom may be the least effective place for transformation to occur unless preservice teachers are required to suffer. The performance exam was a significant experience for the preservice teachers and one in which many did experience suffering, frustration, confusion, and difficulty as well as hope, transformation, and commitment. Even their unresolved frustration with particular issues such as the differences between justice, benevolence, and multiculturalism is a sign of progress rather than failure, as they can now turn toward the interruptions in their experience and in doing so, explore and transform (see English, 2011).

Let the issues raised in class affect you, and let them stir you to be more compassionate. Become an example to your non-Aboriginal preservice teachers, building ongoing relations with Aboriginal people and inviting them to contribute to the course curriculum and to the classroom as teaching colleagues.

Matthew Etherington *is director of The Institute of Indigenous Issues and Perspectives (Canada/Australia/New Zealand) (IIIP) at Trinity Western University. IIIP aims to provide a forum for greater understanding of a broad range of diversity issues pertaining to Indigenous peoples in Canada, Australia, and New Zealand, three countries with similar colonial backgrounds, issues, and Aboriginal policies.*

NOTES

1. Ethics approval was granted in 2012 by the University Ethics Review Board to conduct research on the experiences of fourth-year undergraduate preservice teachers. The student comments in this article have been extracted from this ongoing research.

2. *Siya:m* is a Sto:lo word describing a leader recognized for wisdom, integrity, and knowledge. The role of the Siya:m is to provide both spiritual and personal mentoring to students of Aboriginal descent and act as a liaison between the university and local Aboriginal communities.

3. I give thanks to the following people: the university Siya:m, Patricia Victor; Gail Stromquist; elders Mercy and Josette; Perry Smith; Joe Desjarlais; Karmen Smith-Brillion; Cheri Brown; Jo-Anne (Jo) L. Chrona; and Jonathan Rempel. In order to maintain a regular commitment of speakers to this class in the future, an Institute of Indigenous Issues in Education will be formed to provide stipends.

REFERENCES

Battiste, M. (2013). *Decolonizing education.* Saskatoon, Canada: Purich.

Collins, C., & Nolan, M. (2005). Sites of benevolence. *Journal of Australian Studies, 29*(85), 5–10. Retrieved from http://eprints.qut.edu.au/4603/1/4603_3.pdf

Craven, R. (2003). Shaping a glad tomorrow: Mandatory Indigenous studies teacher education courses as an international educational priority. In M. McInerney & S. Van Etten (Eds.), *Sociocultural influences and teacher education programs* (pp. 165–193). Charlotte, NC: Information Age.

Crowley, B., & Coates, K. (2012). *MLI's Brian Lee Crowley and Ken Coates in iPolitics—Rage and rebirth: The way forward for First Nations.* Retrieved from http://www.macdonaldlaurier.ca/mli%e2%80%99s-brian-lee-crowley-and-ken-coates-in-ipolitics-%e2%80%93-rage-and-rebirth-the-way-forward-for-first-nations/

Denzin, N. K., Lincoln, Y. S., & Smith, L. T. (Eds.). (2008). *Handbook of critical and Indigenous methodologies.* Thousand Oaks, CA: Sage.

Dion, S. (2009). *Braiding histories: Learning from Aboriginal peoples' experiences and perspectives.* Vancouver, Canada: University of British Columbia Press.

Egea-Kuehne, D. (Ed.). (2008). *Levinas and education: At the intersection of faith and reason.* New York, NY: Routledge.

English, A. (2011). Transformation and education: The voice of the learner in Peters' concept of teaching. In S. E. Cuypers & C. Martin (Eds.), *Reading R. S. Peters today* (pp. 123–134). Oxford, United Kingdom: Wiley-Blackwell.

Finney, S., & Orr, J. (1995). "I've really learned a lot, but . . .": Cross-cultural understanding and teacher education in a racist society. *Journal of Teacher Education, 47*(5), 327–333.

First Nations Education Steering Committee. (2010). *New teacher certification requirements benefit Aboriginal learners.* Retrieved from http://www.fnesc.ca/wordpress/wp-content/uploads/2011/03/

Freire, P. (2005). *Pedagogy of the oppressed* (30th ed.). New York, NY: Continuum.

Kanu, Y. (2006, April). *Decolonizing Indigenous education: Beyond culturalism: Toward post-cultural strategies.* Paper presented at the meeting of the American Educational Research Association, San Francisco, CA.

Ladson-Billings, G. (2004). New directions in multicultural education: Complexities, boundaries, and critical race theory. In J. A. Banks & C. A. McGee Banks (Eds.), *Handbook of research on multicultural education* (2nd ed., pp. 2–29). San Francisco, CA: Jossey-Bass.

Lingenfelter, J. E., & Lingenfelter, S. G. (2003). *Teaching cross culturally: An incarnation model for learning and teaching.* Ada, MI: Baker Academic.

Lomawaima, K. T., & McCarty, T. L. (2006). *"To remain an Indian": Lessons in democracy from a century of Native American education.* New York, NY: Teacher's College Press.

Martin, K. L. (2008). *Please knock before you enter: Aboriginal regulation of outsiders and the implications for researchers.* Queensland, Australia: Post Pressed.

McInerney, D. M., & Van Etten, S. (Eds.). (2002). *Research on sociocultural influences on motivation and learning* (Vol. 1). Greenwich, CT: Information Age.

Mill, J. S. (1974). *On liberty.* Gertrude Himmelfarb (Ed.). London, England: Penguin Books. (Original work published 1859).

Miyagawa, M. (2012). A sorry state. In S. Rogers, M. DeGagne, J. Dewar, & G. Lowry (Eds.), *Speaking my truth: Reflections on reconciliation and residential schools* (pp. 175–194). Ottawa, Canada: Aboriginal Healing Foundation.

Nord, W. (2010). *Does God make a difference: Taking God seriously in schools and universities.* New York, NY: Oxford University Press.

Rasmussen, C., Baydala, L., & Shennan, J. (2004). Learning patterns and education of Aboriginal children: A review of the literature. *The Canadian Journal of Native Studies* 24(2), 317–342.

Smith, M. S. (2011, July 7). Equity in Aboriginal education is the only way forward. *Rabble.ca.* Retrieved from http://rabble.ca/news/2011/07/equity-aboriginal-education-only-way-forward

St. Denis, V. (2013). Silencing Aboriginal curricular content and perspectives through multiculturalism: There are other children here. In F. Widdowson & A. Howard (Eds.), *Approaches to Aboriginal education in Canada: Searching for solutions* (pp. 26–37). Alberta, Canada: Brush Education.

Stove, D. (2011). *What's wrong with benevolence? Happiness, private property, and the limits of enlightenment.* New York, NY: Encounter Books.

Tanaka, M. T. D. (2009). *Transforming perspectives: The immersion of student teachers in Indigenous ways of knowing.* Retrieved from ProQuest Dissertations and Theses. (504847261)

Viri, D. (2003). Standards in American Indian/Alaskan Native education: Preparing Native and non-Native teachers for variable contexts. In M. McInerney & S. Van Etten (Eds.), *Sociocultural influences and teacher education programs* (pp. 35–63). Charlotte, NC: Information Age.

Wolterstorff, N. (2008). *Justice: Rights and wrongs.* Princeton, NJ: Princeton University Press.

Reports from the Field

Lessons Learned: Outreach Education in Collaboration with Tribal Colleges

THOMASINE HEITKAMP, LAUREL VERMILLION, KENNETH FLANAGAN, and RANDALL NEDEGAARD

This article describes an undergraduate social work degree offered in two tribal communities through collaboration with tribal colleges, including the accommodations that were made to adjust to the pitfalls of the one-size-fits-all approach commonplace in mainstream higher education. Based on lessons learned in working with the Turtle Mountain Band of Chippewa and the Standing Rock Sioux Tribe, proposed suggestions include a shared mission of outreach education; engagement with stakeholders and elders in development and implementation of the program; collaboration that suspends dominant culture practices to accommodate local educational and program needs; personalized attention to help students overcome barriers; the construction of a community of learners; instructional strategies to ensure student retention; and plans for the additional cost and time.

THE THORNY AND ONGOING problems in Indian Country can be solved.[1] The authors suggest expanding social work education and training programs in tribal communities. In particular, providing a degree-granting social work program to local residents on-site can enhance the ability of tribal communities to solve systemic problems of poverty. The authors' experiences in developing partnerships and collaborations, which resulted in the offering of undergraduate social work programs on tribal lands, are outlined here by explaining seven principles of best practice.

A critical focus of this work is to be more responsive to the need for more trained social workers in tribal communities. The profession of social work is guided by standards and ethical practices that concentrate on enhancing services to diverse populations. These ethical principles promote culturally competent practices for social workers, as highlighted in the Code of Ethics of the National Association of Social Workers (NASW), which states: "Social workers should understand culture and its function in human behavior and society, recognizing the strengths that exist in all cultures" (National Association of Social Workers, 2008, p. 6). This principle requires social workers to practice with cultural humility and allows for the engagement of nonpaternalistic partnerships with communities (Tervalon & Murray-Garcia, 1998). Social workers are also educated to develop and implement social policies that address the needs of vulnerable populations.

Social Work Response

The literature is rife with scholarship that documents the historic inability to reduce economic and health disparities among American Indians and Alaskan Natives (Austin, 2009; Goodkind et al., 2010). The lack of adequate housing and educational support, in addition to unaddressed physical and mental health needs, is thoroughly documented (Austin, 2010; Gone & Trimble, 2012; Jones, 2006; U.S. Commission on Civil Rights, 2003). The United Nations Permanent Forum on Indigenous Issues reports, "[American Indians] live shorter lives, have poorer health care and education, and endure higher unemployment rates" (n.d., p. 1). However, the social work profession has focused on engaging in research activities on tribal lands, according to Yeager (2011), as well as providing support and advancement to academic careers through grant-writing activities to serve tribal nations. Little has been written about nontribal universities offering degrees face-to-face on tribal lands in collaboration with tribal colleges and universities.

The challenges of educating social workers to prepare them to work with American Indians require a critical understanding of the historical trauma experienced by colonized nations (Lyons, 2011). Yellow Bird (2004) describes colonialism as the "invasion, subjugation and occupation of one people by another" (p. 33). As a result, the trauma associated with colonization is a contributing factor associated with the problems facing American Indians (Brave Heart, Chase, Elkins, & Altschul, 2011). Therefore, social work intervention in Indian Country must provide an opportunity to address trauma specific to American Indians. This includes the use of traditional healing practices and ceremonies (Bassett, Tsosie, & Nannauck, 2012). A critical resource for social workers addressing colonialism can be found in the text *Decolonizing Social Work* (Gray, Coates, Yellow Bird, & Hetherington, 2013).

Social Work Education Response

The abovementioned studies highlight the opportunities and challenges for social work in American Indian communities. The Council on Social Work Education (CSWE), the accreditation agency for social work education, responded to this concern by assembling a task force that provided recommendations challenging schools of social work to alleviate this identified workforce shortage (Council on Social Work Education, 2010). The task force found that 489 full-time social work students were identified as American Indian/Alaskan Native in 2007. This limited number of students highlights the need for more American Indian students to enter social work education. Complicating this challenge is the fact that rural areas, where tribal lands are located, generally experience an overall workforce shortage of social workers (Quinn, Phillips, & Heitkamp, 2011; Whitaker, Weismiller, & Clark, 2006). Below is a conceptual lens for collaborative practice based on seven principles, including sharing a mission, engaging stakeholders and tribal elders, suspending dominant cultural practices, personalizing attention, building a community of learners, engaging strategies to increase student retention, and planning for the additional time and costs.

A Conceptual Lens: Nation Building

Brayboy, Fann, Castagno, and Solyom (2012) provide a conceptual lens called "nation building" that can guide collaborative educational practice. The figure below presents a suggested model to better assure success in collaborations among tribal colleges and mainstream universities.

Students enrolled in higher education courses appear at the center of the figure; concentric circles surrounding these students represent the context of working with tribal communities in collaboration with tribal colleges. The subsequent circles represent the critical workforce need for social workers and the commitment of outreach education in the field of social work education. At the outer edge of the circle is the nation-building lens that provides a visual tool to examine the principles surrounding educational endeavors with tribal entities. This schema is versatile and can be used to offer any professional degree, including law, criminal justice, medicine, nursing, and other health care professions.

The constructs of nation building are aligned directly with the values and the premises of social work practice. For example, the principle

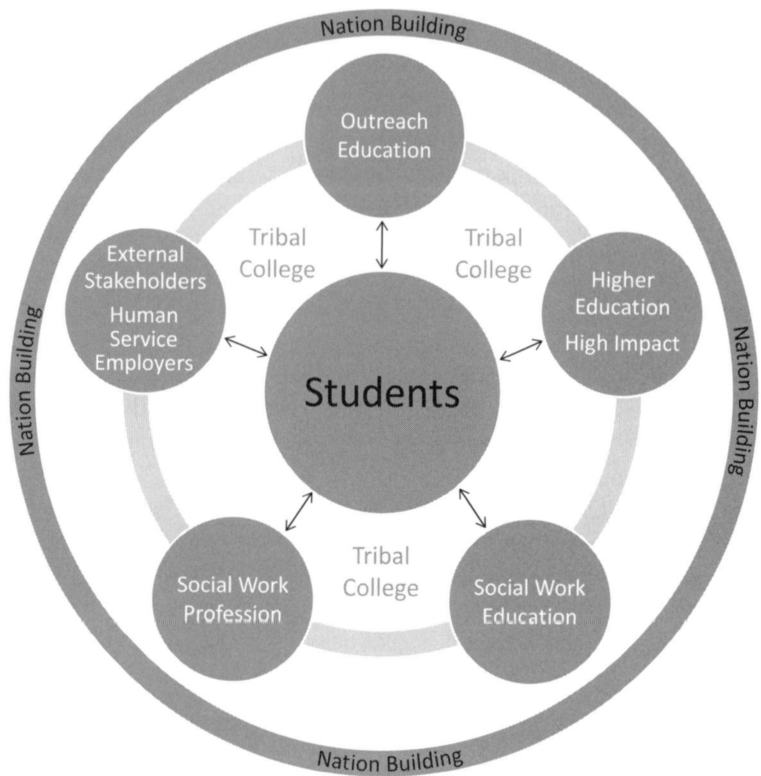

Nation-building schema

of not using a deficit model is aligned with the strength-based model of social work practice, which recognizes and uses personal, environmental, and cultural assets to bring about change (Rapp, Saleebey, & Sullivan, 2006). At the center of the nation-building construct is a focus on the value of self-determination that aligns directly with that social work core value. The NASW has published a primer with indicators to help social workers enhance their professional practice with diverse populations (National Association of Social Workers, 2007). The principles of nation building, in turn, require giving attention to the economic conditions of tribal members, mirrored in a professional social work focus on people in the environment. At the core is the need for a commitment to broaden access to higher education, which is critical to providing the skills and credentials to advance the well-being of tribal nations. Therefore, using social work best practices and lessons learned in collaborations are central to the constructs of both nation building and good social work educational practice.

Collaborations With Tribal Colleges and Universities

Historical examples of collaborations with tribal colleges and universities (TCUs) include activities such as faculty exchanges, development of articulation agreements, experiential learning, and joint degree development (Nichols, Baird, & Kayongo-Male, 2001). This article, however, describes collaborations that move beyond exchanges to offering social work degrees. Because TCUs are typically full-service institutions with basic education courses, childcare centers, access to fitness centers, and other community resources, they are a key resource that combines personal attention with cultural relevance to assist American Indians in overcoming educational barriers.

Most importantly, collaborations with TCUs safeguard against a Eurocentric pedagogy and an institutional organization burdened by bureaucratic approaches. Hierarchical approaches tend to be less successful in program development and implementation, especially in Indian Country (e.g., Shotton, 2012). In their study designed to assess what works in successful partnering and collaboration between state universities and tribal colleges, Nichols et al. (2001) found that:

> While engaging in collaborations with good intention seems simple enough, the research revealed several levels of complexity stemming from historical, cultural, political, economic, and even geographic factors. Disregarding these complexities had negative effects on some of the partnerships and the participants. Good faith intentions were not enough in some instances. (p. 3)

Meaningful collaborations with TCUs and tribal communities require that mainstream campus leadership, faculty, and staff acknowledge and accommodate the unique cultural and language attributes of tribal communities. Tribal communities do not place the same value on hierarchy and rigidity that is typically valued on mainstream campuses. Instead, they value informality and flexibility (Badwound & Tierney, 1988). Weaver (2000) confirmed the necessity of a holistic approach to educational practices. She found that a disruption of harmony and balance by insensitive educational practices led to dissonance and negative experiences toward education. Instructors must, therefore, be attuned to the value of balance and strive to build personal trust through thoughtful, consistent, and fair educational approaches.

Recognition among social work educators that significant economic barriers exist for American Indian students in securing advanced degrees is critical. Sorkness and Kelting-Gibson (2006) noted that the culture of poverty must be understood, along with American Indian culture, when offering education programs. Financial constraints are major factors affecting enrollment in higher education (McAfee, 1997; Wilder, Jackson, & Smith, 2001). A CSWE task force report commented on the potential barriers to higher education for Native American students:

> For example, geographical distance from a social work program, isolation factor, need of survival skills to succeed in mainstream culture, need for support/reference groups, and lack of mentoring programs are critical. Distance education may be a good alternative for many Native American students. (Council on Social Work Education, 2010, p. 35)

Distance education programs hold promise as a delivery method but only if they are designed to address the specific needs of students and are sufficiently culturally responsive. The technology required in online course offerings can overmediate interactions and hamper the establishment of meaningful relationships. Tribal college collaborations assist in mediating these educational issues. TCUs can also guarantee that students have access to the supports that family and traditional ceremonies provide. TCU collaboration, then, addresses the geographical isolation that inhibits access to mainstream higher education among American Indian students living in tribal communities.

In an effort to reduce these challenges, increase access to higher education, and provide culturally sensitive educational programs, the University of North Dakota (UND) collaborated with two tribal colleges to provide two on-site bachelor of social work programs. A description of each program follows.

In 2009, the Department of Social Work had nine students who secured a bachelor's degree in social work from UND by completing course work offered by faculty at Turtle Mountain Community College (TMCC). Eight alumni accepted employment in their tribal communities upon graduation. Important lessons learned, based on this collaboration, include: (1) the need for increased flexibility; (2) the importance of devoting significant administrator, staff, and instructor time to planning and preparation; (3) the fact that the use of technology to deliver the program off-campus was not as effective as in other distance programs, requiring faculty to travel to TMCC to teach portions of the curriculum; and, (4) the necessity of face-to-face interaction in advisement and instruction.

Using lessons learned from TMCC, the Department of Social Work began a collaboration with Sitting Bull College (SBC) in fall 2012, offering courses on-site on a part-time basis. SBC primarily serves the Standing Rock Sioux Tribe, which is more than 300 miles from UND. Students who are enrolled have typically completed the associate degree in human services from SBC and have matriculated into this program to secure their bachelor's degree in social work (BSW) from UND.

Notably, President Barack Obama visited the Standing Rock Sioux Tribe in Fort Yates in June 2014 to stress the importance of a greater dialogue about the needs in Indian Country. The dramatic needs of people who live in the communities within this tribal nation were the rationale for choosing this location. The president's visit and the subsequent media coverage increased attention to problems in Indian Country throughout the United States.

Seven Principles Based on Best Practices

The authors describe seven basic principles used in developing and delivering the program, the pitfalls, and the necessary accommodations required in working with tribal colleges to deliver a degree-granting program, based on past experiences. Each principle is reviewed below in the context of the authors' experiences.

Shared Mission of Outreach Education

The mission of the Department of Social Work at UND is "to prepare competent, responsive and ethical social workers who empower vulnerable populations, promote social justice and are committed to serving diverse populations" (University of North Dakota, 2012). The BSW program supports this mission by "providing students with the knowledge, values and skills for generalist social work, with an emphasis on culturally responsive practice in rural communities" (University of North Dakota, 2012). Offering the BSW to members of the Standing Rock Sioux Tribe at SBC and to the Turtle Mountain Band of Chippewa at Turtle Mountain Community College demonstrated a strong commitment to fulfilling the mission of the Department and the BSW program and its program goals. The mission of serving tribal communities requires a flexibility and openness to address complex administrative challenges, including enrollment, financial aid issues, and registration. The formal university system has multiple layers of bureaucracy that are not amenable to these complex collaborations. In addition, the formal system is typically not nimble enough to focus on students' unique ethnic and cultural heritage. These limitations must be addressed.

Active efforts were made by the authors to ameliorate concerns surrounding the lack of adequate educational and support services to the students enrolled in SBC. Ultimately, a single support person was assigned to work exclusively with the program to guarantee continuity. The support of the president at UND was critical. He ensured that people in key leadership positions at UND supported the program. He worked collaboratively with leaders at SBC, which was a critical element to safeguard the success of the program (e.g., Martin, 2005; McClellan, Tippeconnic-Fox, & Lowe, 2005).

Fully Engaging Stakeholders/Tribal Elders in Development and Implementation

The BSW degree is offered by UND to students at the community college. However, at the tribal college students live in a community environment that is intimately involved in their day-to-day lives. To offer a program that is culturally responsive, the lead author actively consulted traditional community leaders and elders regarding many aspects of program implementation, and they assisted by recruiting students. Community leaders included officials and instructors at the tribal college, directors of social service agencies, officials at the Bureau of Indian Affairs, the Tribal Council, the local media, and UND alumni. Faculty, administrators, and staff mounting tribal college programs on-site must be present in these communities and engaged in active listening for the community, not just for the enrolled students. Any message, either directly or indirectly, that devalues the role of tribal elders will destroy trust. Different elders may hold different types of knowledge; therefore, becoming acquainted with a significant number of elders is important. Female elders, as well as male elders, should be included in all the conversations, as the traditional roles of men and women differ dramatically. When an elder's voice and support has been included, support is attainable. However, when consensus cannot be reached, the existence of diverse viewpoints must not be allowed to paralyze action. For example, at a key point in recruitment, an elder encouraged an author from UND to be less timid and more confident in making decisions.

The recruitment approach, therefore, is very different from UND's main campus. Multiple meetings and participation at career fairs and other traditional gatherings on-site provided opportunities to interact directly with prospective students and promote the program. The sheer distance from campus, especially for the SBC program, and problems with early contract negotiations created barriers that were challenging to overcome in the early stages of development. However, once trust was developed, the program was easily launched. Again, trust is developed by a physical presence in the community.

Collaboration That Suspends Dominant Cultural Practices

Collaborations with the TCUs were necessary for the many reasons described above. Students enrolled in tribal colleges are accustomed to more personalized service and instruction, which required UND to provide more personal attention to TMCC and SBC students than it typically offers to UND students, as well as an advocate to express student needs. Ultimately, this increased attention to recruitment and retention allowed for better coordination that focused on improving student participation and persistence (McClellan et al., 2005). If administration, faculty, and staff cannot make clear financial and time commitments for creating success, the program will fail.

An early tension at SBC included the fear of siphoning off the best students from the tribal college's associate of arts degree in human services. To address this legitimate concern, the UND Department of Social Work chair developed an academic grid outlining how the tribal college classes would fulfill the requirements of the BSW curriculum. The UND Registrar's Office honored the General Education Requirements Transfer Agreement in transfer of credits. As a result, students were able to move through the social work program in a more timely and seamless manner.

The use of appropriate textbooks that describe, in a respectful manner, the experience of working and living in Indian Country is necessary for successful collaboration. Instructors have a responsibility to address textbooks that are Eurocentric in their approach. Additionally, students and faculty have the capacity to use online resources and articles that supplement textbook materials. A growing number of excellent books are written by American Indian authors or individuals who know firsthand about the traditional ways, culture, values, and language of American Indian people. Teaching in tribal communities forces mainstream faculty to examine textbook materials through a different lens.

Personalizing Attention to Help Students Overcome Barriers

To help guarantee that no one slips through the cracks, a single point of contact for students is required. The authors suggest that on-site advisement be offered. Additionally, an academic plan must be in place that provides each student an opportunity for program completion at an appropriate time. Once an agreement is developed to offer courses listed in the academic plan, follow-through is critical. The commitment from UND officials to honor previous academic work at the tribal college to fulfill general education/essential studies requirements is critical for retention and program completion. Flexibility on transfer of credits to fulfill requirements is necessary to limit loan debt and ensure retention. For example, a beading class can fulfill the art requirement in the same way as a main campus ceramic arts class. Similarly, a class on the Lakota language will fulfill the same requirement as a Norwegian language class on the UND campus.

Faculty who are American Indian can best establish relationships in Indian Country, but a significant barrier to the SBC/TMCC collaboration is that the Department of Social Work does not employ any American Indian full-time faculty who can serve as mentors and provide more cultural familiarity. The CSWE report describes the importance of hiring more Native American faculty, and the CSWE report indicates there are only 48 full-time Native American faculty in social work education (Council on Social Work Education, 2010). Because of this limited pool of potential PhD American Indian instructors, American Indians with master of social work (MSW) degrees should be recruited to teach whenever possible.

Building a Community of Learners

The tribal college program offered by UND uses a cohort model, with students completing classes on Fridays and Saturdays at SBC and in the evenings at TMCC. On-site teaching of small classes provides an opportunity to build a community of learners and for professors to interact with students on both a group and an individual basis. However, rigidity within this approach can disadvantage students who need to step out of the cohort for a bevy of reasons, so adjustments must be made for opportunities for individual instruction.

The focus on a community of learners allows students to share resources. The extreme weather conditions in this area often cause car battery failure, thus students need to carpool from their homes in the remote rural areas of the tribal communities. Also, a request was honored not to host classes on Friday evenings because community celebrations occur around sporting activities on those nights, which students wish to attend. The class schedule was adjusted to accommodate this need at the SBC site.

Instructional Strategies to Increase Student Retention

The retention of students is perhaps the single most important challenge that mainstream higher educational institutions face. The Department of Social Work chair and the BSW director identified multiple challenges prior to implementing the first class session, and others were quickly determined after teaching began. Reyhner (1992) reviewed research to identify seven school-based reasons why American Indian students drop out of school. Four of these reasons directly or indirectly address instructional methods:

1. The perception that teachers do not care about Native students
2. Passive "transmission" teaching methods
3. Inappropriate curriculum designed for mainstream America
4. Large schools that present students with an impersonal education

These four areas were specifically targeted by the program, which led to several changes to the curriculum, teaching styles, and program administration in order to maximize retention.

Additionally, competitive instructional practices that are inherent in Western higher education protocols do not have the same value in American Indian culture. Gilliland (1999) described the importance of emphasizing students' strengths and respecting students. This includes integrating American Indian culture into the curriculum to honor students' pride in their heritage. Instructional practices, therefore, must be adapted to accommodate culture with an understanding of traditional and less traditional students (Cleary & Peacock, 1998).

Instructors must respect the need for students to strive for harmony and balance in their lives.

The teaching style, or method used to transmit learning, has a significant effect on student retention outcomes (Swisher & Deyhle, 1992, p. 90). In the past, professors have delivered lectures for the majority of the class time with limited opportunity for student input through discussion or experiential exercises (Wingfield & Black, 2005). The instructional approach used in the tribal college program included the use of oral traditions, such as storytelling, recommended by Hoffman (1992). Student collaborative learning and the use of oral traditions brought the concepts of social work theory and practice to life. This guaranteed the infusion of course content that was transferable to daily life and students' existing work in the human services field.

The cohort model described earlier works well for American Indian students because it encourages group work versus individual work, and it fits nicely with the values of generosity and humility. Group work allows students to boast about each other instead of themselves; bringing attention to oneself is frowned upon in many American Indian cultures. This approach was advanced in planning and program delivery.

Another means of measuring whether instructors engage in culturally appropriate instructional practices is to assess students' perceptions of teaching effectiveness through the use of formative evaluations (Angelo & Cross, 1993). Students completed summative course evaluations for every course offered, assessing how well instructors connected ideas to real-world situations and whether they treated students with respect. These instructor ratings were used as part of yearly performance evaluations and were made available to department leadership to confirm that no concerns existed.

Planning for Cost and Time Commitment

Higher education programs are costly to administer. A commitment to provide programs away from campus to a small number of students contradicts the standard university model that values larger class sizes to offset costs. Two faculty members spent 2 days on the road and 2 days teaching a small number of students at SBC. Given that SBC is located more than 300 miles from campus, this was a significant commitment of windshield time. The TMCC program also required extensive travel to a location more than 180 miles away from UND's main campus. Faculty volunteered their weekend time away from their families to provide instruction. They drove on icy roads, accommodated the multiple challenges students faced, adjusted their teaching styles, and so on. Without a doubt, the strength of this program has been the commitment of faculty and the open and transparent communications with the tribal college officials and students.

An additional cost was the commitment of time for faculty to attend training, which occurred prior to launching the SBC program. The training provided instruction on the culture of the Standing Rock Sioux Tribe and best practices in teaching in collaboration with TCUs.

Conclusion

The seven principles described above have proven effective in the authors' experiences. No doubt, other programs have varying experiences, and sharing lessons learned and ongoing challenges is vital for appropriate intercultural examination. Although social work education has not been responsive to the needs of tribal communities, the TCUs provide a model that is based on serving communities in a culturally responsive manner. However, in spite of rhetoric about a commitment to diversity in mainstream higher education, little progress has been made, and very few programs are able to claim any significant measure of improvement (Guillory & Wolverton, 2008). Retention of American Indian students requires a commitment to move beyond the platitude of engaging in endless planning with no results. To do this, university recruitment offices must be willing to adopt an assessment process that addresses the needs of the students, not the institution.

These case studies demonstrate two successful experiences by one social work department and two tribal colleges. The commitment by leadership, faculty, and staff to deliver these programs was a fundamental ingredient in program delivery. The support of upper administration at UND and the TCUs was necessary. Additionally, reestablishing trust among community tribal members, which enabled forgiveness of the inevitable missteps, proved key to success.

The authors strongly suggest that institutions of higher learning examine practices that fail to serve students from diverse populations and firmly commit to include underserved populations rather than making policy decisions primarily based on financial considerations. A principal factor is the training of faculty in ways to better serve American Indian students and the hiring of American Indian faculty.

Finally, the success of the programs described above is based on the ability to expand capacity among the TCUs. Part of the strategic plan at SBC, developed in fall 2014, is for the tribal college to offer its own undergraduate social work degree. UND officials have agreed to serve as consultants in program development and implementation, including help with the writing related to accreditation standards. SBC administrators understand the ongoing need for trained social workers and plan to respond locally.

Thomasine Heitkamp *is professor of social work at the University of North Dakota.*

Laurel Vermillion *(Seen-by-Her-Nation; Hunkpapa-Lakota) has served as the president of Sitting Bull College since 2006.*

Kenneth Flanagan *is associate professor of social work at the University of North Dakota.*

Randall Nedegaard *is assistant professor and MSW director in the Department of Social Work at the University of North Dakota and primary instructor for the collaborative Bachelors of Science Social Work program with Sitting Bull College.*

NOTE

1. The authors are sensitive to different perspectives in the use of terms to describe Indigenous populations. For purposes of this article, the term *American Indian* is used, unless referencing other authors' materials, in which the term *Native American* is the preference.

REFERENCES

Angelo, T., & Cross, P. (1993). *Classroom assessment techniques: A handbook for college teachers* (2nd ed.). San Francisco, CA: Jossey-Bass.

Austin, A. (2009). *American Indians and the Great Recession.* Washington, DC: Economic Policy Institute.

Austin, A. (2010). *Different race, different recession.* Washington, DC: Economic Policy Institute.

Badwound, E., & Tierney, W. G. (1988). Leadership and American Indian values: The tribal college dilemma. *Journal of American Indian Education, 28*(1), 9–15.

Bassett, D., Tsosie, U., & Nannauck, S. (2012). "Our culture is medicine": Perspectives of Native healers on posttrauma recovery among American Indian and Alaska Native patients. *The Permanente Journal, 16*(1), 19.

Brave Heart, M. Y. H., Chase, J., Elkins, J., & Altschul, D. B. (2011). Historical trauma among indigenous peoples of the Americas: Concepts, research, and clinical considerations. *Journal of Psychoactive Drugs, 43*(4), 282–290.

Brayboy, B. M. J., Fann, A. J., Castagno, A. E., & Solyom, J. A. (2012). Postsecondary education for American Indian and Alaska Natives: Higher education for nation building and self-determination. *ASHE Higher Education Report, 37*(5), 1–154.

Cleary, L. M., & Peacock, T. D. (1998). *Collected wisdom: American Indian education*. Needham Heights, MA: Allyn & Bacon.

Council on Social Work Education. (2010). *Task force on Native Americans in social work education*. Washington, DC: Author.

Gilliland, H. (1999). *Teaching the Native American*. Dubuque, IA: Kendall/Hunt.

Gone, J. P., & Trimble, J. E. (2012). American Indian and Alaska Native mental health: Diverse perspectives on enduring disparities. *Annual Review of Clinical Psychology, 8*, 131–160.

Goodkind, J. R., Ross-Toledo, K., John, S., Hall, J. L., Ross, L., Freeland, L., & Lee, C. (2010). Promoting healing and restoring trust: Policy recommendations for improving behavioral health care for American Indian/Alaska Native adolescents. *American Journal of Community Psychology, 46*(3/4), 386–394.

Gray, M., Coates, J., Yellow Bird, M., & Hetherington, T. (2013) *Decolonizing social work*. Surrey, United Kingdom: Ashgate.

Guillory, R. M., & Wolverton, M. (2008). It's about family: Native American student persistence in higher education. *The Journal of Higher Education, 79*(1), 58–87.

Hoffman, E. (1992). Oral language development. In J. Reyhner (Ed.), *Teaching American Indian students* (pp. 132–142). Norman: University of Oklahoma.

Jones, D. S. (2006). The persistence of American Indian health disparities. *American Journal of Public Health, 96*(12), 2122–2134.

Lyons, S. R. (2011). Actually existing Indian Nations: Modernity, diversity, and the future of Native American studies. *The American Indian Quarterly, 35*(3), 294–312.

Martin, R. G. (2005). Serving American Indian students in tribal colleges: Lessons for mainstream colleges. *New Directions for Student Services, 109*, 79–86.

McAfee, M. E. (1997). *From their voices: American Indians in higher education and the phenomenon of stepping out* (Unpublished doctoral dissertation). Colorado State University, Fort Collins.

McClellan, G. S., Tippeconnic-Fox, M. J., & Lowe, S. C. (2005). From discussion to action. *New Directions for Student Services, 109*, 95–98.

National Association of Social Workers. (2007). *Indicators for the achievement of the NASW Standards for Cultural Competence in Social Work Practice*. Retrieved from http://www.socialworkers.org/practice/standards/naswculturalstandardsindicators2006.pdf

National Association of Social Workers. (2008). *Code of ethics of the National Association of Social Workers*. Retrieved from http://www.socialworkers.org/pubs/code/code.asp

Nichols, T. J., Baird, P., & Kayongo-Male, D. (2001). Partnerships offer promise and perils: A study of collaborations with state universities. *Tribal College Journal, 13*(2), 20–23.

Quinn, A., Phillips, A., & Heitkamp, T. (2011). *North Dakota social workforce report*. Retrieved from https://www.nursing.und.edu/social-work/_files/nd-swk-workforce-report.pdf

Rapp, C. A., Saleebey, D., & Sullivan, W. P. (2006). The future of strengths-based social work. *Advances in Social Work, 6*(1), 79–90.

Reyhner, J. (1992). American Indians out of school: A review of school-based causes and solutions. *Journal of American Indian Education, 31*(3), 37–56.

Shotton, H. (2012, December 12). A state of emergency for American Indian and Native students. *The Huffington Post*. Retrieved from www.huffingtonpost.com/heather-shotton/native-indian-education_b_2288074.html

Sitting Bull College. (2014). *About us*. Retrieved from www.sittingbull.edu/aboutus/vision/

Sorkness, H. L., & Kelting-Gibson, L. (2006, February). *Effective teaching strategies for engaging Native American students*. Paper presented at the Annual Meeting of the National Association of Native American Studies, Baton Rouge, LA. Retrieved from http://www2.ed.gov/rschstat/research/pubs/oieresearch/conference/sorkness_200602.pdf

Swisher, K., & Deyhle, D. (1992). Adapting instruction to culture. In J. Reyhner (Ed.), *Teaching American Indian students* (pp. 81–95). Norman: University of Oklahoma.

Tervalon, M., & Murray-Garcia, J. (1998). Cultural humility versus cultural competence: A critical distinction in defining physician training outcomes in multicultural education. *Journal of Health Care for the Poor and Underserved, 9*(2), 117–125.

United Nations Permanent Forum on Indigenous Issues. (n.d.). *Economic and social development*. Retrieved from http://undesadspd.org/IndigenousPeoples/ThematicIssues/Economicandsocialdevelopment.aspx

University of North Dakota. (2012). *Bachelor of science in social work student handbook, 2012–2013*. Grand Forks, ND: Author.

U.S. Commission on Civil Rights. (2003). *A quiet crisis: Federal funding and unmet needs in Indian Country*. Retrieved from www.uscrr.gov/pubs/na0703/na0731.pdf

Weaver, H. N. (2000). Culture and professional education: The experiences of Native American social workers. *Journal of Social Work Education, 36*(3), 415–428.

Whitaker, T., Weismiller, T., & Clark, E. J. (2006). *Assuring the sufficiency of a frontline workforce: A national study of licensed social workers*. Retrieved from http://workforce.socialworkers.org/studies/nasw_06_execsummary.pdf

Wilder, L. K., Jackson, A. P., & Smith, T. B. (2001). Secondary transition of multicultural learners: Lessons from the Navajo Native American experience. *Preventing School Failure, 45*(3), 119–124.

Wingfield, S. S., & Black, G. S. (2005). Active versus passive course designs: The impact on student outcomes. *Journal of Education for Business, 81*(2), 119–123.

Yeager, D. (2011). Developing Native American expertise in social work. *Social Work Today, 11*(6), 8. Retrieved from http://www.socialworktoday.com/archive/092011p8.shtml

Yellow Bird, M. (2004). Cowboys and Indians: Toys of genocide, icons of colonialism. *Wicazo Sa Review, 19*(2), 33–48.

Contributor Information

The *Journal of American Indian Education* (*JAIE*) is a refereed journal publishing original scholarship about the education issues of American Indians, Alaska Natives, Native Hawaiians, and Indigenous peoples worldwide, including First Nations, Māori, Aboriginal/Torres Strait Islander peoples, Indigenous peoples of Latin America and Africa, and others. *JAIE* strives to improve Indigenous education through empirical research; knowledge generation; and transmission to researchers, communities, and diverse educational settings.

JAIE encourages dialogues among researchers and practitioners through research-based articles elucidating current educational issues and innovations. *JAIE* also invites original scholarly essays advancing a point of view about an educational question or issue when supported by cited research literature; original reviews of literature in underexplored areas; original expository manuscripts that develop or interpret a theory or issue; and Reports from the Field. Studies grounded in Indigenous research methodologies are especially encouraged.

Prepare manuscripts according to the most recent *Publication Manual of the American Psychological Association* (6th ed.) (http://www.apastyle.org/manual/index.aspx). Format manuscripts in Microsoft Word and blind for anonymous peer review; manuscripts not blinded or appropriately formatted will be returned. Authors must certify that the manuscript is not being considered by another publisher. All empirical studies must document: (1) the use of accepted ethical protocols for research with human subjects; and (2) site-specific approvals, including research and/or institutional review board approvals required by Native nations, tribes, or bands as well as schools and school districts, where appropriate. Please use the term most appropriate to the Indigenous group or people to whom the manuscript refers. *American Indian/Alaska Native, Native American, Native Hawaiian,* and *Indigenous* are acceptable terms when referring to Indigenous peoples of the United States.

All manuscripts must be submitted electronically to jaie@asu.edu. Submit the double-spaced manuscript as one Word document (do not send a pdf), including the title and abstract (150 words); biographical statement(s) for each author (50 words each); and contact information for each author, including author name, affiliation, e-mail address, physical street address, and phone number. Do not include author name(s) on or in the manuscript.

Feature-length Manuscripts Original scholarly manuscripts should be double-spaced, 7,500–8,000 words total, including endnotes, if any, and references.

Reports From the Field Original scholarly manuscripts providing descriptive, evaluative, and/or policy-oriented analyses of innovative education models and practices may be considered as "Reports From the Field." Reports should be up to 5,000 words, including endnotes, if any, and references. See the website and *JAIE* 49 (3) for a full description of "Reports From the Field."

Manuscripts will be considered throughout the year and, if accepted, will be published in any of the three issues at the direction of the editorial staff. There is no remuneration for *JAIE* contributors; authors will receive three free copies of the issue in which the manuscript is published. For more information, see the *JAIE* website at https://jaie.asu.edu/

JOURNAL OF AMERICAN INDIAN EDUCATION

CALL FOR PEER REVIEWERS

AS A PEER-REVIEWED JOURNAL, *JAIE* depends upon the generosity of our colleagues in the field of Indigenous education. Rigorous, constructive, and supportive peer review is essential to the health of our field and to the quality of our journal.

We invite interested academic colleagues, practitioners, and advanced doctoral students to sign up as peer reviewers for *JAIE*. Your name will be added to the database we consult for reviews of submitted manuscripts. *JAIE* uses double-blinded peer review: the identities of manuscript authors are not shared with reviewers, and the identities of peer reviewers are not shared with authors. If you are already a reviewer for the journal, please log on to the new website and fill out a Reviewer Application so we have updated information in our database.

The responsibilities of peer review include:

- Timely response to requests to review, letting the editorial assistant know if you can review the submitted manuscript
- Completion of review within three to four weeks of receiving the manuscript
- Detailed commentary on the strengths and weaknesses of the manuscript, including its contribution to knowledge, adherence to ethical standards of research, narrative and organizational coherence, and relevance of analytic or descriptive content
- Constructive and supportive suggestions to improve or enhance the manuscript.

To sign up, please visit the *JAIE* website at https://jaie.asu.edu/. At the foot of the home page, click on Reviewer Application. Fill out the fields of the online form, attach a PDF copy of your c.v., and click Submit.

Thank you!